Having Your Say

HAVING YOUR SAY

Threats to Free Speech in the 21st Century

EDITED BY J. R. SHACKLETON

with contributions from

PHILIP BOOTH · NICK COWEN · STEPHEN DAVIES
CLAIRE FOX · DENNIS HAYES · VICTORIA HEWSON
LEO KEARSE · JACOB MCHANGAMA
DAVID S. ODERBERG · J. R. SHACKLETON

Institute of
Economic Affairs

First published in Great Britain in 2021 by
The Institute of Economic Affairs
2 Lord North Street
Westminster
London SW1P 3LB
in association with London Publishing Partnership Ltd
www.londonpublishingpartnership.co.uk

The mission of the Institute of Economic Affairs is to improve understanding
of the fundamental institutions of a free society by analysing and expounding
the role of markets in solving economic and social problems.

A CIP catalogue record for this book is available from the British Library.

ISBN 978-0-255-36800-1

Many IEA publications are translated into languages other
than English or are reprinted. Permission to translate or to reprint
should be sought from the Director General at the address above.

Typeset in Kepler by T&T Productions Ltd
www.tandtproductions.com

Printed and bound by CPI Group (UK) Ltd, Croydon, CR0 4YY

CONTENTS

ABOUT THE AUTHORS

Philip Booth

Philip Booth is Professor of Finance, Public Policy and Ethics at St. Mary's University, Twickenham, and Director of the Vinson Centre and Professor of Economics at the University of Buckingham. He is Senior Academic Fellow at the Institute of Economic Affairs. He is also a Senior Research Fellow in the Centre for Federal Studies at the University of Kent and Adjunct Professor in the School of Law, University of Notre Dame, Australia. Philip is a Fellow of the Royal Statistical Society, a Fellow of the Institute of Actuaries and an honorary member of the Society of Actuaries of Poland.

Nick Cowen

A political scientist with interests in political theory, law and public policy, Nick Cowen studied for his BA in Philosophy at University College London and also has an MPhil in political theory from Oxford University. He wrote his doctoral dissertation at King's College London on the political economy of distributive justice. Nick became a Fellow at the NYU School of Law in 2018.

Stephen Davies

Steve Davies is Head of Education at the Institute of Economic Affairs. From 1979 to 2009 he was Senior Lecturer in the Department of History and Economic History at Manchester Metropolitan University. He has also been a Visiting Scholar at the Social Philosophy and Policy Center at Bowling Green State University, Ohio, and a Program Officer for the Institute for Humane Studies in Arlington, Virginia. His many publications include *Empiricism and History* (Palgrave Macmillan, 2003) and *The Wealth Explosion: The Nature and Origins of Modernity* (Edward Everett Root, 2009).

Claire Fox

Claire Fox is Director of the Academy of Ideas, which she established to create a public space where ideas can be contested without constraint. She convenes the yearly Battle of Ideas festival and initiated the Debating Matters Competition for sixth-formers. In May 2019, she was elected to the European Parliament as an MEP for the North West England constituency. In 2020, she was made an honorary professor at the University of Buckingham. In September 2020, Claire became a member of the House of Lords as Baroness Fox of Buckley.

Dennis Hayes

Dennis Hayes is an emeritus professor of education at the University of Derby and the Director of the campaign group Academics for Academic Freedom. He sits on the advisory board of The Free Speech Union. In 2006–7 he was the first (joint) president of the University and College Union (UCU). Among his many publications is the controversial and best-selling book, co-authored with Kathryn Ecclestone: *The Dangerous Rise of Therapeutic Education*. First published in 2009, the book was reissued, with a new preface, in 2019 as a Routledge Education Classic.

Victoria Hewson

Head of Regulatory Affairs at the Institute of Economic Affairs, Victoria Hewson is a practising solicitor. She has specialised in commercial, technology and data protection matters across a range of sectors. Victoria has published a number of papers for the IEA, and writes regularly for the *Telegraph* and *CityAM,* and appears on television and radio to discuss trade and regulatory policy.

Leo Kearse

Leo Kearse is a Scottish comedian and writer, based in London. He is part of a new wave of raw, bold, American-inspired comedians taking the big UK clubs by storm, and was Scottish Comedian of the Year in 2017–18. A self-styled 'right wing comedian', his 'Extinction Rebellion' video went viral, selling out shows throughout the UK. He is also popular abroad, with 2019 seeing him perform in twenty countries. Among various credits, Kearse has written for BBC shows including *Breaking The News, Mock The Week* and *The Mash Report*. He played Mick Fleetwood in the ITV drama *Breaking The Band: Fleetwood Mac*.

Jacob Mchangama

Jacob Mchangama is the founder and executive director of Justitia and a visiting fellow at the Foundation for Individual Rights in Education in Washington. In 2018 he was a visiting scholar at Columbia's Global Freedom of Expression Center. He has commented extensively on free speech and human rights in outlets including the *Washington Post*, the *Wall Street Journal*, *The Economist* and *Foreign Affairs and Foreign Policy*. Jacob has published in academic and peer-reviewed journals, including *Human Rights Quarterly*, the *American Journal of Political Science* and *Amnesty International's Strategic Studies*. Jacob is the host and narrator of the podcast Clear and Present Danger: A History of Free Speech and the author of a forthcoming book on the history of free speech from Socrates to Zuckerberg (Basic Books and Basic Books UK, 2022).

David S. Oderberg

David S. Oderberg, Professor of Philosophy at the University of Reading, completed his doctorate at Wolfson College, the University of Oxford. He has written four books and edited or co-edited five others, as well as being the author of over sixty academic papers. His main research areas are metaphysics and ethics. In 2013 David delivered the Hourani Lectures in Ethics at the State University at the Social Philosophy and Policy Center, Bowling Green University, Ohio. In 2016 he was named as one of the fifty most influential living philosophers.

J. R. Shackleton

Professor of Economics at the University of Buckingham, and Research and Editorial Fellow at the Institute of Economic Affairs, Len Shackleton was educated at King's College, University of Cambridge, and the School of Oriental and African Studies. He has run two business schools and worked as an economist in the UK Civil Service. Len has published widely in academic and policy journals on labour market issues and is a regular contributor to written and broadcast media. He has authored or edited twelve books and edits *Economic Affairs,* the academic journal published by the IEA and the University of Buckingham.

SUMMARY

- Free speech is, with free trade, freedom of enterprise and security of property, one of the key features of classical liberalism. It is currently being undermined, for a variety of plausible reasons, by government, social and mainstream media companies, and the behaviour of individuals, firms and non-profit organisations.
- Having thrown off the obvious shackles on free speech in the 1960s and 1970s, we are now imposing new forms of restriction on freedom of thought and expression. Young people in particular are being socialised into a censoriousness about dissident behaviour and speech which is reminiscent of totalitarian regimes.
- One reason for suppressing free speech is concern with 'hate crimes'. But speech bans have a long history, which shows that, whatever the intent, they are often more likely to hurt disadvantaged groups than protect them. Recent restrictions on speech in western Europe, for example, have been copied to sinister purpose by oppressive governments.
- Political extremism is more widespread, but less dangerous, than is often supposed by mainstream politicians and commentators. The way to tackle it

is by intelligent policing to restrict opportunities for violence rather than by blanket bans on freedom of expression.

- The presence of disturbing online content is leading governments towards increasing regulation of social media and Internet hosts. But the attempt to eliminate disinformation and harm from the Internet is likely to be doomed to failure. Recent legislative proposals will not achieve what they are intended to achieve, but may cause innovation and competition to suffer.

- Free speech is considered by both right and left as negotiable or even dispensable when faced with issues such as Covid-19 or Black Lives Matter. In such circumstances our political elites pursue a particular narrative through mainstream and social media and effectively 'cancel' those who express opposition or even mild doubt.

- The prevailing mood of political correctness inhibits comedians and makes people ashamed of what they or their parents used to laugh at in the past. While the consensus may be that there have to be some externally imposed limits on comedic speech, we can't assume that those who police this speech will act reasonably. A healthy society needs to be able to laugh at itself, even if it occasionally hurts.

- A neglected area of concern is 'commercial free speech' – what advertisers can and can't say. UK advertising is widely praised worldwide, and a major export earner. But it is increasingly restricted both by government bans and by the Advertising Standards Authority, an

unrepresentative body which promotes a form of
social engineering and has called for the regulation of
political speech.

- Some aspects of religious freedom are under threat.
Public Space Protection Orders and Community
Protection Notices have been activated against
Christian activists handing out leaflets and holding
placards or even silently praying in anti-abortion
demonstrations. Proselytising Christians have also
been investigated for alleged hate crimes, while some
people have lost their jobs for asserting Christian
values. Muslims are also particularly at risk from anti-
extremist policies.

- Universities, like other organisations, have the right
to prohibit certain types of expression and behaviour
from their premises, and impose contractual
obligations on employees. However, recent challenges
to free speech in higher education, often driven by
radical students demanding suppression of ideas, 'no
platforming' and sanctions against or dismissal of
staff, are a worrying phenomenon. A major part of the
problem is the lack of institutional diversity in higher
education.

- Trade unions, in the past among the fiercest
proponents of free speech, have moved away from
this and instead focus on a 'therapeutic' role which
requires them to protect members from speech that is
felt to threaten harm or vaguely defined 'offence'.

- 'Offence' has indeed been too widely accepted as a
reason for speech restrictions. People may *feel* offended

without *being* offended in a significant way, and even those being offended may suffer no meaningful harm. And while people can be compensated for harm from free speech, there is no way of compensating people for removing the freedom to speak. In any case, on purely pragmatic grounds it is nearly always best to allow serious disagreements to be vigorously debated rather than suppressed.

1 INTRODUCTION

J. R. Shackleton

The twenty-first century offers people more opportunities than ever before in history to communicate ideas and opinions. Thirty or forty years ago a relative handful of privileged individuals – senior politicians, trade union leaders, television personalities, published authors and columnists – had a regular national or international platform via television or newspapers. A rather larger number had access to pulpits, lecture theatres, public meetings or hustings. The bulk of the population, though, was largely confined to talking to relatives, friends and neighbours. The more determined might write letters to newspapers or their political representatives. Some particularly committed individuals might collect signatures for a petition, or organise a demonstration. Others, though, lapsed into apathy – or worse, despairing of their lack of influence or voice, might resort to violence and terrorism.

Today, however, technological developments allow us all to make our views known via social media, online comments pages, blogs and YouTube. An ordinary person – for example, the late Captain (then Sir) Tom Moore[1] – can rise from obscurity to mass acclaim in days. Others can set up their own websites and lucratively promote ideas and their own personalities as bloggers or influencers. Politicians and fundraisers can send personalised messages to millions of individuals in nanoseconds. Individuals can research issues online in greater depth and with far less effort than previous generations could ever have dreamt of. And we can take part in real-time discussions about these issues with people anywhere in the world via apps such as Zoom.

Generations have fought for the right for their voices to be heard, often suffering harsh penalties for their temerity in expressing such an aspiration. This surely ought to be a Golden Age for free speech, a technological triumph for democracy.

New types of speech restrictions

Yet this doesn't seem to be the case. The liberating new technologies and the freedoms associated with them have provoked a reaction which is leading to growing restrictions on speech.

Much of this, of course, comes from the state. For example, the concept of 'hate crime' – unknown in UK law until 1998 – has expanded from its origin as an aggravating

---

1   In April 2020 Tom Moore, approaching his 100th birthday, began to walk 100 laps of his garden in aid of National Health Service charities. Within weeks he had become a celebrity, attracted over 1.5 million individual donations, and was knighted by the Queen.

factor in mainly violent crime to a catch-all category where the potential for causing harm or offence, in real life or online, is now causing well over 100,000 hate crimes[2] (plus the even broader category of hate 'incidents') to be reported each year. These numbers have been boosted by the increasing range of categories of protected individuals, and will likely be increased further by new legislation in Scotland (where the Hate Crime and Public Order Bill[3] sets out a new crime of 'stirring up hatred', which even includes private speech within the home) and England and Wales (where the Law Commission[4] has consulted on proposals which include criminalising football chants).

Government restrictions on speech cover many other areas, with varying degrees of justification, from terrorism-related material to child pornography to adverts for junk food. Whatever the objections of libertarians, at least such restrictions go through a process of parliamentary debate.[5] However, there is also increasing pressure on social media to ban content of which governments and pressure groups disapprove. Facebook, Twitter and the rest usually

2 Home Office, Hate Crime, England and Wales, 2019 to 2020 (https://www.gov.uk/government/statistics/hate-crime-england-and-wales-2019-to-2020).

3 The Bill was passed in March 2021. Hate Crime Bill passed (www.gov.scot).

4 Law Commission: Hate Crime (https://www.lawcom.gov.uk/project/hate-crime/).

5 Although powers are often delegated to bodies whose workings are not subject to significant parliamentary scrutiny. For example, Ofcom, the communications regulator, now forbids broadcasters to transmit 'hate speech', which it defines much more widely than 'hate crimes'. Ofcom Broadcasting Code Section 3 (https://www.ofcom.org.uk/tv-radio-and-on-demand/broadcast-codes).

acquiesce as they fear that they would otherwise face new legislation.

Social media occupy an anomalous position in our society. Sold originally as a 'public square' where all could meet and communicate, they avoided the restrictions placed on orthodox publishers. Yet in practice their owners have felt obliged, under pressure from politicians and public outrage, to ban certain types of written and audiovisual content. As private organisations, they have a right to do so. Yet Twitter, Facebook and YouTube exercise huge market power, and their interventions are often seen as arbitrary.

Was it reasonable for Twitter to ban then US President Donald Trump for incendiary remarks in the last days of his Presidency? Many think so, but many think not. Few may lament Facebook's bans on holocaust denial[6] and QAnon[7] conspiracy theories, but quite where the line is to be drawn is unclear. There are pressures to ban climate change 'denial'[8] (a vague category, which might well ensnare legitimate scientific or economic concerns), while the Royal Society and the British Academy[9] have called for social media companies to 'remove harmful information and punish those who spread misinformation' about Covid-19 vaccination. This call was taken up in January

---

6   Facebook bans Holocaust denial content. BBC News, 12 October 2020.

7   Facebook bans all QAnon groups as dangerous amid surging misinformation. Reuters, 6 October 2020.

8   Climate denial ads on Facebook seen by millions, report finds. *The Guardian*, 8 October 2020.

9   Vaccine hesitancy threatens to undermine pandemic response. British Academy, 10 November 2020.

2021 when YouTube removed TalkRadio from its platform, apparently because interviewees or callers had queried government lockdown policy.[10]

These are controversial areas and the danger of blanket restrictions is that legitimate concerns and new evidence which runs counter to scientific consensus will be banned alongside more obviously crazy or malevolent content. It is not surprising that many now feel that social media should be regulated or even broken up if they are going to use their power in such ways.

There is a long history of restrictions forced on the media of the day – books, newspapers, the theatre, cinema, broadcasting – by government. What is very new is the downside of the democratisation of the means of communication – Twitterstorms of online invective against people or institutions who have transgressed, or are thought to have transgressed, rapidly changing social norms and mores.

It has always been the case that a degree of mutual hostility lies beneath the surface of complex societies. But technology has empowered people to express this hostility much more easily, much more rapidly, and at little cost to themselves.

Some have dismissed these eruptions of unpleasantness as transgressors 'getting what they deserved' or abuse to be shrugged off on the principle that, though sticks and stones may break their bones, names will never hurt them. Many are particularly happy to see those who have

---

10 After an uproar, YouTube rescinded its ban. TalkRadio reverses decision to ban channel. BBC News, 5 January 2021 (https://www.google.co.uk/amp/s/ www.bbc.co.uk/news/amp/technology-55544205).

achieved any degree of status or celebrity pulled down. But this is surely an ignoble sentiment, often based on envy. It ignores the human cost to real individuals and their families. This cost is held to be justified by trumpeting some abstract principle, or to address theoretical offence given to some abstract group or 'community'. It also dismisses the future restraints which this places on the free speech of others who, although not particularly sympathetic to the individuals penalised by the online mob, may be inhibited from expressing any opinion at all for fear of giving offence to somebody.

Such inhibition may be class- and generation-based. Those who went to university and are acquainted with metropolitan thinking, or simply have fewer miles on the clock, may be able to negotiate the ever-changing rules of discourse and come out with the appropriate banalities. Others, like the unfortunate Greg Clarke, former chairman of the Football Association, are not so nimble. Clarke was forced to resign for clumsy speech such as describing footballers of colour as 'coloured'.[11] Or remember the Cambridge college porter and former Labour councillor Kevin Price,[12] whose dismissal was demanded by students for refusing to support a council motion which included the words 'trans women are women': how many college porters or other working-class individuals with similar doubts about transgenderism will dare to voice them in future?

---

11 Greg Clarke resigns as FA chairman after comments on 'coloured footballers'. *The Independent*, 10 November 2020.

12 The trans debate could cost this Cambridge porter his job. *The Spectator*, 27 October 2020.

Transgenderism is the hottest of hot potatoes for anybody these days, notwithstanding other credentials they may have acquired for feminist and socialist sympathies, as Harry Potter author J. K. Rowling[13] has discovered. This is an example of the way in which some protected statuses appear to override others, as black actor and committed Christian Seyi Omooba found when she was sacked from a theatre production because of anti-gay views she had tweeted six years previously[14] – an example, incidentally, of the expanding field of 'offence archaeology', where statements made years ago in a different context are disinterred to attack people today.

The obloquy which results from speaking out against the consensus is too often unmitigated by protection from our great 'liberal' institutions, such as universities, newspapers and charities, which sometimes seem only too eager to agree with demands for people's heads for opinions which would have caused nobody to bat an eyelid in the recent past. In its supine response to student pressure, Cambridge University rescinded its visiting fellowship invitation to Jordan Peterson[15] while *The Guardian* newspaper failed to stand by its longstanding

---

13 J. K. Rowling criticised for 'condescending' and 'transphobic' tweets. Sky News, 8 July 2020.

14 Ms Omooba subsequently appealed to an employment tribunal, lost, and was ordered to pay £300,000 legal costs. Seyi Omooba: actress sacked over anti-gay post must pay legal costs. BBC News, 31 October 2021.

15 Cambridge University rescinds Jordan Peterson invitation. *The Guardian*, 20 March 2019.

columnist Suzanne Moore[16] in the face of staff opposition to her views. Numerous universities dissociated themselves from historian David Starkey[17] after he made ill-considered remarks about slavery in a YouTube discussion with Darren Grimes – a contretemps which also involved a heavy-handed though thankfully ultimately abortive police intervention.

The growing influence of Black Lives Matter has also led to sackings of people who disagree with its approach: Charity CEO Nick Buckley[18] lost his job after criticising BLM as 'post-modern, neo-Marxists' who are 'call[ing] for the destruction of Western Democracy and our way of life', while football fan Jake Hepple[19] was sacked for flying a 'White Lives Matter' banner over Burnley's ground in protest at 'taking the knee' at the start of Premier League games.

What may be particularly worrying is that it takes relatively small numbers 'calling out' some hapless individual for offending orthodoxy to cause institutions to cave in. The power of social media is such that within minutes several thousand people with little better to do may dive into some dispute, even though they have given the matter little thought and may represent a tiny minority of all

16 Suzanne Moore leaves *Guardian* months after staff send letter of revolt over 'transphobic' content. *Press Gazette*, 22 March 2019.

17 David Starkey loses two university positions after saying slavery didn't constitute genocide. *The Independent*, 3 July 2020.

18 Charity boss fired after criticising Black Lives Matter. *The Critic*, 2 July 2020.

19 Burnley fan Jake Hepple sacked for part in 'White Lives Matter' banner. Sky Sports, 24 June 2020.

those potentially concerned with the event. Craven executives are unwilling to defend themselves, their staff or their clients for fear of the online mob's attention being redirected at them. Long ago John Stuart Mill (2006: 10) warned against the 'tyranny of the majority'[20]; now, perhaps, it is the hyperactive minority which exercises a new type of tyranny.

In longer perspective, today's restrictions on free speech and penalties against speech transgressions may seem trivial. After all, nobody is burnt at the stake any longer for their religious principles, or imprisoned for demanding a wider franchise. Books are not banned by the government; no Lord Chamberlain vets plays before they can be staged. Swear words and simulated sex on television are *de rigueur*, while Lord Alfred Douglas's 'love that dare not speak its name' is rarely silent today. And of course you can be just as rude as you like about Boris Johnson or Nigel Farage on *Mock the Week*. Compared with China, or Iran, or dozens of similarly hellish polities, we have it very easy.

But there is a growing sense that, having thrown off the obvious shackles on free speech in the 1960s and 1970s, we are now insidiously imposing new, and in some ways more worrying, restrictions on freedom of thought and expression. Upcoming generations are aware that they have to be very careful what they say in public or post online so as not to offend anyone and run the risk of wrecking their career or facing criminal penalties. Films, plays and

---

20 Mill argued that it was the 'tyranny of the prevailing opinion and feeling' rather than specifically political oppression which was the problem in Victorian England.

books produced in the past are suspect, and must be accompanied by trigger warnings; now-offensive words and phrases must be removed or bleeped.

And young people are increasingly being socialised, at school, university and at work, into a censoriousness about dissident behaviour, speech or thought which is not a million miles – though perhaps in a different way and with less obvious drabness – from that of the former East Germany or Soviet Union.

This book

Much of this concern is widely shared. In this book, however, we aim to go beyond generalised concern to look at the issue of twenty-first-century free speech in greater depth. Although a number of themes necessarily recur in these essays, each represents a distinct voice and a novel angle on the threats to free speech.

We begin with a chapter from Jacob Mchangama, who puts today's demands for the suppression of hate speech into historical context. Looking at key episodes in the history of free speech, he argues that speech bans are more likely to hurt disadvantaged groups than benefit them. Censorship and repression was a key component in the systemic subjugation of African-Americans, and black South Africans under apartheid. Iconic champions of freedom and equality such as Fredrick Douglass, Martin Luther King, Mahatma Gandhi and Nelson Mandela all relied on the practice and principle of free speech even while it was often denied. Mchangama also examines how debate over the United Nations Declaration of Human Rights and the legally binding International Covenant on Civil and Political Rights was hijacked by the Soviet Union and its allies. The requirement for member states to prohibit 'national, racial or religious hatred' was subsequently used to punish human rights activists and religious believers challenging communist rule. More recently, countries such as Belarus and Turkey have copied human rights laws in Western Europe and turned them to their own advantage against dissidents. Mchangama concludes that laws against hate speech 'chart a dangerous course for minorities they are intended to protect'.

Nick Cowen's chapter argues for a tolerance of political extremism, which he claims to be far more widespread but rather less dangerous than people often suppose. Cowen rejects the idea that classical liberals should exempt 'everyday extremism' from the presupposition in favour of free speech. In practice legal definitions of extremism often capture people who represent no danger to anybody. Drawing from the example of the English Defence League, as well as the political left, he suggests that many people attracted to *violent* extremism are in reality not particularly ideologically driven, but are more interested in the excitement of physical confrontations. The core leadership of extremist movements tries to attract recruits by offering opportunities for group-sanctioned violence against minorities and political opponents. Using intelligent policing to deprive them of those opportunities is likely to be more successful than censorship of extreme views.

In her chapter Victoria Hewson notes that concern over online content is leading governments in the UK and the EU towards increasing regulation. But the attempt to eliminate disinformation and harm from the Internet seems likely, she argues, to be doomed to failure. Measures such as the EU's Code of Practice on Disinformation and the proposals in the UK's Online Harms White Paper are not going to achieve what they intend, but they could mean loss of trust in institutions and reductions in freedom of expression and association. There will also, Hewson points out, be economic costs if innovation and competition suffer as a consequence.

Claire Fox points out that, across the political spectrum, free speech is considered second order, a 'negotiable and dispensable nicety'. It is easily ignored when society faces major crises, among which she includes the Covid-19 pandemic. She draws attention to the way in which our political elites have pursued a particular narrative about the pandemic, and systematically excluded or demonised dissident opinion. In a similar way, the identity narrative highlighted by the Black Lives Matter movement is driven by elites who push unconscious bias training, mandate how we are allowed to speak and 'cancel' those who express opposition or even mild doubt or reticence. Fox asserts that the historically feeble commitment to free speech by both left and right means that censorship has too easily become the default position. We need, she says, a new movement committed to trusting the public and to seeing our fellow citizens as equal to the task of discerning their own views by guaranteeing access to unlimited, freely expressed ideas – however dangerous they may seem to elite opinion.

One of the effects of increasing restrictions on free speech is to inhibit today's comedians and make people ashamed of what they or their parents used to laugh at in the past. While this may be kinder to minorities in our diverse society than some of the comedy of the 1970s, there are dangers in stifling our sense of humour. In his chapter, self-described 'right-wing comedian' Leo Kearse outlines the long history of comedy censorship. While discussing such extreme incidents as the *Charlie Hebdo* murders, he also describes his own experience of being banned from venues and denounced on social media. He points out that self-censorship is key to his own work and that of other successful comedians. Knowing what is appropriate at different types of gig is the comedian's responsibility; there are no hard and fast rules. While the consensus may be that there have to be externally imposed limits of some kind on comedic speech, Kearse says we can't assume those who want to police this speech will act fairly. A healthy society needs to be able to laugh at itself, even when it hurts. Comedy has the power to break down barriers between people, but if comedians have to tiptoe around these barriers, will they ever be destroyed?

In my own contribution, I examine the case for free speech in advertising or 'commercial speech'. Advertising is heavily regulated by government in the UK, but also by supposedly voluntary restrictions determined by the Advertising Standards Authority (ASA), a body funded by advertisers. I review the analysis of Ronald Coase, who was sceptical of the distinction between 'good' and 'bad' advertising which economists from Alfred Marshall to Nicholas

Kaldor had drawn, and which provides an apparent rationale for regulation. Coase argued that there can be no hard and fast distinction between free intellectual speech and free commercial speech; similar rules should apply to both. I also point out that the ASA has gone far beyond its original remit of trying to ensure that advertising be 'legal, decent, honest and truthful'. In censoring attitudes and behaviours which can be portrayed in advertisements, it is now part of a wider paternalistic and neo-puritan project which arguably operates outside adequate democratic scrutiny.

Philip Booth is concerned about the way in which Public Space Protection Orders (PSPOs) and Community Protection Notices are being used to restrict freedom of speech, conscience and prayer. He particularly draws attention to those Christians who oppose abortion, although he fears that adherents of other religions (or no religion) could be affected by disturbing legal precedents which have been established. In his chapter he describes the way in which PSPOs have been used against activists giving out leaflets, holding placards or even silently praying, and argues that such activities do not transgress Mill's harm principle, which is frequently used to justify government restrictions on free speech. Booth also discusses incidents where proselytising Christians have been investigated for alleged hate crimes, the Northern Ireland case where bakers were prosecuted for refusing to decorate a cake with a slogan in support of gay marriage, and actual or threatened dismissals from jobs for asserting Christian values. He concludes that government officials and the police have been given, or taken, powers to undermine freedom of speech and conscience which have no place in a free society.

Stephen Davies offers a subtle discussion of free speech which goes beyond abstract platitudes to consider the role of property rights and institutions. He points out that any organisation has the right to prohibit certain types of expression within its own premises, or to use freely accepted contracts to restrict employees' freedom of speech in the course of the employer's business. However, catch-all prohibitions against 'bringing the organisation into disrepute' by private activities outside the workplace are more problematic. Davies then considers the application of these ideas to the university. Although historically universities have seen themselves as defenders of orthodoxy (for instance, only those prepared to assent to the Anglican faith were allowed to be members of Oxbridge colleges), since early in the twentieth century they were seen as arenas of freedom of expression and dissent. Recent challenges to free speech in higher education, often driven by radical students who demand suppression of certain ideas, sanctions against or dismissal of staff and the creation of 'safe spaces' where speech is controlled, are a worrying phenomenon. Davies sees part of the problem lying in the fact that largely government-funded universities are too much alike, and argues for greater diversity of institutions rather than expecting them all to conform to a politically correct norm. He also argues that current problems of free speech within universities are not unique to these institutions, but are rather just one manifestation of wider conflicts between populist conservatism and radical leftism which are evident in the mainstream and social media and within charities, quangos, the public sector and large private businesses.

In his contribution, Dennis Hayes decries the way in which trade unions, in the past among the fiercest proponents of free speech, have moved away from this and instead focus on a 'therapeutic' role which requires them to protect members from speech that is felt to threaten them or cause (vaguely defined) offence. A former president of the University and College Union, he believes the UCU now completely misunderstands academic freedom. It is not simply about academics' right to teach and discuss their subject without management interference, but includes the freedom of speech for people – staff, students and guests – with whose opinions you may profoundly disagree and regard as offensive.

In the final chapter, the philosopher David Oderberg conducts a forensic examination of widely used terms such as 'offence', 'insult' and 'harm'. He argues that 'offence' has been too widely accepted as a reason for curtailing free speech. People may *feel* offended without *being* offended in a significant way, and even those being offended may suffer no meaningful harm. Oderberg points out that, while people can be compensated for harm arising from free speech, there is no way of compensating people for the removal of freedom to speak. He detects logical flaws and hypocrisy in many arguments for suppression of free speech and asserts that in any reasonable order of priorities within a democratic society, the positive right to speak must outweigh the negative right to avoid offence. This is because the entire democratic process is predicated on the freedom of all citizens to speak in matters of politics and anything that may feed into political decision-making, such as culture and social norms. This absolute legal freedom would be compatible with public discouragement of genuinely offensive speech. It would also be consistent with the banning of some speech on private platforms as long as the integrity of the democratic process was not seriously undermined. Oderberg concludes that even on purely pragmatic grounds it is best to allow serious disagreements between people to be vigorously debated; the alternative of suppressing free speech is always far less attractive.

Our authors, then, come from different perspectives and different disciplines. Readers may not share their viewpoints. Nevertheless all the authors offer informed and considered insights on the importance of free speech, which together with free trade, freedom of enterprise and security of property, is one of the central features of classical liberalism. As ever, the Institute of Economic Affairs does not endorse the opinions of particular authors but as an educational charity seeks to increase understanding of the institutions of a free society. In a world where ever-proliferating means of having your say are matched by ever-proliferating excuses for preventing you doing so, such understanding is vital.

2 A HISTORY OF LAWS ON HATE AND ABUSE

Jacob Mchangama

The past decade has seen a sharp drop in respect for civil liberties, according to *The Economist*'s *Democracy Index*. No liberties 'have deteriorated as much as ... freedom of expression and media freedom'. This includes substantial deteriorations in Western Europe (EIU 2020). Part of this free speech recession is driven by European liberal democracies intent on fighting 'hate speech' with significant collateral damage for important political, religious and artistic speech due to the inherent vagueness and majoritarian bias of hate speech bans.

French President Emmanuel Macron (2018) has warned that '[o]ur governments, our populations will not tolerate much longer the torrents of hate coming over the Internet'. In 2019 Angela Merkel told the German Bundestag that '[f]reedom of expression has its limits. Those limits begin where hatred is spread ... where the dignity of other people is violated'. The war on hate speech is not limited to talk. *The Times* reported that more than 3,300 people – or around nine people a day – were arrested in the UK in 2016 as part of a police effort 'to combat social media hate speech'.[1] On 23 April 2020 the Scottish Government presented its Hate Crime Bill, which includes new offences of 'stirring up hatred' based on age, disability, race, religion, sexual orientation, transgender identity and variations in sex characteristics.[2] Following non-binding EU initiatives, France and Germany have imposed 'intermediary liability' for social media networks, who must remove hate speech within 24 hours.[3]

These European governmental initiatives seem to have had an impact on the content moderation policies of US-based private social media platforms. Facebook deleted 26.9 million pieces of content for violating its Community Standards on 'hate speech' in the last quarter of 2020. That's nearly seventeen times the 1.6 million instances of deleted 'hate speech' in last quarter of 2017.[4]

---

1   Police arresting nine people a day in fight against web trolls. *The Times*, 12 October 2017 (https://www.thetimes.co.uk/article/police-arresting-nine -people-a-day-in-fight-against-web-trolls-b8nkpgp2d).

2   Hate Crime Bill, Scottish Government, 23 April 2020 (https://www.parlia ment.scot/-/media/files/legislation/bills/current-bills/hate-crime-and -public-order-scotland-bill/introduced/bill-as-introduced-hate-crime -and-public-order-bill.pdf). This has now been passed into law, as noted in the Introduction.

3   France threatens big fines for social media with hate-speech law. *Wall Street Journal*, 13 May 2020 (https://www.wsj.com/articles/france-threatens-big -fines-for-social-media-with-hate-speech-law-11589398472?mod=e2tw). Germany's online crackdowns inspire the world's dictators. *Foreign Policy*, 6 November 2019 (https://foreignpolicy.com/2019/11/06/germany-online -crackdowns-inspired-the-worlds-dictators-russia-venezuela-india/).

4   Community Standards Enforcement Report, February 2021 (https://trans parency.facebook.com/community-standards-enforcement).

Given the long and bloody history of religious, ethnic and racial intolerance in Europe and the US, equality and non-discrimination are vital goods constituting cornerstones of liberal democratic societies. These goods are challenged when minority groups are subject to hatred and bigotry, which can ultimately result in emotional harms and can even damage mental health.[5] However, by targeting hate speech through various forms of censorship, European democracies are presuming that free speech and equality are conflicting rather than mutually supportive values. The idea that free speech is a hindrance to equality and a vector of racism is also prevalent among those who protest against racism and police brutality towards minorities following the killing of George Floyd, an African-American man, by the police in Minneapolis in May 2020. Several newspaper editors have been fired for publishing opinions deemed hurtful to victims of racism, just as streaming services such as Netflix have removed 'offensive' content, e.g. the 1939 classic *Gone with the Wind*.

There are compelling reasons to be sceptical of this logic. Several authors have pointed out the lack of empirical evidence that hate speech laws constitute an effective remedy against purported harms such as hate crimes (e.g. Strossen 2018: 121ff, 133ff). Critics have also pointed out that restrictions of 'hate speech' punishing 'bad tendencies' rather than imminent harm are inherently vague, which creates a risk of targeting important criticism and

---

5   Who gets to define what's 'racist'? *Contexts*, 15 May 2020 (https://contexts .org/blog/who-gets-to-define-whats-racist/).

dissent. This 'bad tendency' rationale essentially vests enforcers with unfettered discretion, and is the Achilles heel of contemporary laws, which allow hateful speech to be punished despite the absence of imminent harm (Strossen 2018; Walker 1994; Shiell 2019; Mchangama 2011; Heinze 2016). Moreover, restrictions on free speech – even when formally neutral – will tend to perpetuate and entrench the values of the dominant in-group and marginalise out-groups.

These criticisms of hate speech bans are not merely abstract and theoretical. They have strong historical support. And, as I hope to show, key episodes in the history of free speech support the notion that hate speech bans are more likely to *hurt* than to benefit minorities and disadvantaged groups, and that a commitment to robust free speech protections has been indispensable for remedying systematic discrimination and oppression.

Suppression of abolitionist writings in the US

In 1835, Northern abolitionists began an organised campaign to end American slavery by sending publications to white Southerners. The abolitionist campaign was met with vitriolic opposition by Southern states which adopted laws prescribing harsh penalties – including flogging and hanging – for publishing and distributing abolitionist writings (Curtis 2000: 128–29, 293–94). Not unlike social media companies today, Southern postmasters were obliged to screen the mail for abolitionist writings and prevent their circulation. Southern politicians even demanded a federal law against abolitionist writings and that Northern states punish anti-slavery opinions, although these initiatives failed.

Southern congressmen did manage to push through the 'Gag Rule' in 1836, prohibiting the presentation of anti-slavery petitions in Congress until its repeal in 1844. Southerners used several different justifications for the censorship of 'fanatic and incendiary' abolitionist speech (Curtis 2000: 153). These included the idea of group libel. Senator John C. Calhoun of South Carolina complained that the abolitionist petitions 'contained reflections injurious to the feelings of himself, and those with whom he was connected' (Curtis 2000: 176). He and his constituents refused to be 'deeply, basely and maliciously slandered'.[6] Southern politicians also argued that abolitionist speech would create 'discontent' leading to violent rebellion, even if criticism of slavery did not directly incite to revolt and rebellion. As one commentator argued: 'The unavoidable consequences of [abolitionist] sentiments is to stir up discontent, hatred, and sedition among the slaves' (Curtis 2000: 135). In other words, the 'bad tendency' of abolitionist speech was sufficient grounds for suppression, even in the absence of any imminent harm, and it essentially prohibited transmission of anti-slavery opinion in the South.

Only a robust commitment to free speech ideals among Northerners prevented suppression of abolitionist ideas at the federal level as well as in Northern states. This was often motivated by constitutional principle rather than

6   Cong. Globe, 24th Congress, 1st Sess., 3rd vol. (1836): 77.

sympathy with abolitionists, who were frequently despised as 'fanatics' even by polite opinion in the North. But both mainstream Northern opinion and abolitionists argued that pro-slavery ideas should be free to circulate in the North and that in a free exchange the case for slavery would be defeated. The runaway slave and abolitionist Frederick Douglass became a famous orator and writer, and central to his political philosophy was the idea that 'the right of speech is a very precious one, especially to the oppressed'.[7] In 1860 he wrote a plea for free speech in Boston after an anti-slavery meeting in Boston was disrupted by mob violence:

> Slavery cannot tolerate free speech. Five years of its exercise would banish the auction block and break every chain in the South. They will have none of it there, for they have the power. But shall it be so here? ... A man's right to speak does not depend upon where he was born or upon his color. The simple quality of manhood is the solid basis of the right – and there let it rest forever.[8]

Douglass's insistence on the intimate link between free speech and equality was taken up by a number of individuals and groups which fought the systematic discrimination against African-Americans under 'black codes' and Jim Crow laws in the South after the abolition of slavery and

---

7   The Kansas–Nebraska Bill, speech at Chicago, 30 October 1854.

8   Frederick Douglass's 'Plea for freedom of speech in Boston', 9 December 1860 (https://lawliberty.org/frederick-douglass-plea-for-freedom-of-speech-in -boston/).

well into the second half of the twentieth century. These included the American Civil Liberties Union (ACLU) and the National Association for the Advancement of Colored People (NAACP). Having seen how free speech restrictions tended to hurt minorities and progressive groups, the ACLU and (after some wavering) the NAACP did not pursue the idea of promoting racial equality through hate speech or group libel laws. In the words of Samuel Walker, 'the principal strategy for advancing *group* rights came to be the expansion of constitutionally protected *individual* rights' (Walker 1994: 16), which included repudiating free speech restrictions based on bad tendencies. This strategy led to a cascade of landmark Supreme Court cases expanding First Amendment freedoms, providing a prominent platform for mobilising the American people and securing a 'civil rights revolution' empowering African-Americans.

British colonialism

In the early nineteenth century British political radical speech was routinely suppressed by laws against seditious and blasphemous libel. But reforms in the 1830s and 1840s removed most obstacles to political and religious speech in Britain. John Stuart Mill wrote that the working class had thrown off the yoke of 'paternal' government when they were taught to read and had access to newspapers and political tracts (Mill 1909).

Formally, Britain was committed to exporting its liberal values. *Encyclopædia Britannica* declared that '[i]n the British colonies the press is as free as it is in England'.

The reality was very different. In the colonies race and ethnicity replaced class as the basis of policing speech when
anti-colonial movements began agitating against British
imperial rule.

In India, sweeping prohibitions against sedition and
the promotion of 'feelings of enmity or hatred between
different classes of Her Majesty's Subjects' were adopted
(Acharya 2015).[9] In 1908 the nationalist leader Bal Gangadhar Tilak wrote a number of newspaper articles arguing that a lethal terrorist attack was the regrettable but
natural consequence of British rule.[10] Tilak was convicted
and sentenced to six years of transportation for sedition
and 'promoting enmity between communities'.[11]

India's most famous champion of independence was
also punished for his words. According to Mahatma Gandhi (1921), the freedoms of speech and association were
'the two lungs that are absolutely necessary for a man to
breathe the oxygen of liberty'. But in 1922, Gandhi was sentenced to six years in prison for encouraging non-violent
resistance to British rule. At his trial he made a rousing
speech in favour of free expression (Gandhi 1922):

---

9   The primary source is the Indian Penal Code of 1860, sec. 124A (added by
    Act 27 of 1870, sec. 5); sec. 153A (added by the Indian Penal Code Amend-
    ment Act 4 of 1898, sec. 5), in *Government of India, The Unrepealed General
    Acts of the Governor General in Council: 1834–67*, 3rd edn (Calcutta: Office of
    the Superintendents of Government Printing, India, 1893), 1: 273, 279.

10 Second Tilak Trial-1909, Bombay High Court (https://bombayhighcourt.nic
    .in/libweb/historicalcases/cases/Second_Tilak_Trial_-1909.html).

11 *Emperor v. Bal Gangadhar Tilak* (1908) 10 BOMLR 848 (https://indiankanoon
    .org/doc/1430706/); The second coming of sedition. *The Wire*, 18 February
    2016 (https://thewire.in/law/the-second-coming-of-sedition).

> Affection cannot be manufactured or regulated by law. If
> one has no affection for a person or system, one should
> be free to give the fullest expression to his disaffection,
> so long as he does not contemplate, promote or incite to
> violence.

Though Gandhi was convicted for sedition rather than hate speech, his eloquent defence of free speech serves as a warning against all content-based restrictions punishing bad tendencies. Unless punishments for speech are limited to promoting imminent harm, such as clearly inciting violence, they can be abused to silence political dissent.

As anti-colonial movements gained traction, British officials started operating a parallel system of censorship based on race. In 1918 the British governors in the Caribbean were specifically instructed to intercept and prevent the circulation of anti-colonial writings sent to 'negroes' under their jurisdiction. In 1927 the Secretary of State for the colonies circulated a secret memo (Newell 2016: 68) stressing the need to censor material that could:

> arouse undesirable racial feeling by portraying aspects
> of the life of any section of His Majesty's subjects which,
> however innocent in themselves, are liable to be mis-
> understood by communities with other customs and
> traditions.

This parallel system also applied to the cinema. Censors relied on guidelines issued by the British Board of Film

Censorship. These prohibited depicting 'antagonistic or strained relations between white men and the coloured population of the British Empire'. In Hong Kong these were expanded to include 'showing the white man in a degrading or villainous light' and 'racial questions, especially the intermarriage of white persons with those of other races' (Newman 2013: 167). Contemporary supporters of hate speech laws may argue that the racist free speech restrictions of colonial Britain represent the very oppression they want hate speech laws to prevent. But it is worth remembering that at the time Britain was seen as the world's preeminent liberal state, whose values were widely admired. Accordingly, Britain's censorship of anti-colonial movements should serve as a powerful reminder that even in the most enlightened countries laws punishing the bad tendency of speech are likely to reflect and protect majoritarian biases at the expense of unpopular groups whose ideas might be seen in a very different light by later generations.

Apartheid South Africa

Censorship and suppression were fundamental features of South African apartheid. The Publications Act banned 'undesirable' publications including ones thought to harm relations between groups, and those that brought any section of the community into 'ridicule or contempt' (de Lange 1997).

While formally neutral and aimed at equality between all groups of the South African population, these

provisions were really aimed at preserving white supremacy, the defining feature of apartheid. As the chairman of
an official censorship body explained (de Lange 1997: 23):

> The Appeal Board has emphasized that the South African
> community in no way wants to suppress criticism against
> whites or the government, but writers should realize that
> they are on delicate ground and that they have to make
> sure that what they publish does not assume the charac-
> ter of a hateful attack on the white man.

Not surprisingly, many works were banned for subjecting
whites to ridicule or contempt. Nobel Prize winner Nadine
Gordimer's *Burger's Daughter* was initially banned because
it 'contain[ed] various anti-white sentiments'. *Roots*, the
American mini-series on slavery, was banned in 1984 'as
a substantial number of likely viewers would identify with
the cause of the oppressed American slaves' (Coetzee 1990:
12). Portrayals of 'sexual intercourse between White and
Coloured persons [if] represented to the public as normal,
natural, satisfying and right' were also banned (de Lange
1997: 25).

American abolitionists and civil rights activists had
been able to appeal to and ultimately rely on constitutional freedoms couched in universalist terms. Anti-colonialist
movements within the British empire could point to the
chasm between colonial censorship and Britain's liberal
traditions, which included a commitment to freedom of
thought and speech going back to the abolition of prior
censorship in 1695. But no such legal or ideological support

was available to the opponents of apartheid. The South African Constitutions of 1961 and 1983 contained no Bill of Rights and explicitly discriminated on the basis of race, entrenching apartheid.

This hampered the ability to use free speech as a weapon against apartheid. In fact, the systematic denial of free speech and inability to challenge white supremacy peacefully lay at the heart of the ultimate decision of the leadership of the African National Congress (ANC) to aim to achieve its goals by force. At his infamous Rivonia Trial in April 1964, Nelson Mandela delivered an iconic defence of liberty explaining why the ANC had turned to armed resistance (Mandela 1964):

> All lawful modes of expressing opposition to [white supremacy] had been closed by legislation, and ... we had either to accept a permanent state of inferiority, or to defy the Government. ... We first broke the law in a way which avoided any recourse to violence; when this form was legislated against, and when the Government resorted to a show of force to crush opposition to its policies, only then did we decide to answer violence with violence.

Mandela's speech contains a powerful indictment of the idea that speech restrictions serve to secure social peace and limit violence. Indeed, free speech may be seen as the antithesis of violence, since it allows the peaceful airing of grievances, while censorship may serve to radicalise those who are silenced.

The United Nations, human rights and hate speech

The history of drafting and enforcing UN treaties concerning free speech reaffirms yet again that even well-intentioned 'hate speech' bans empower government officials to suppress any speech they disfavour, including human rights advocacy. After the end of World War II, the new United Nations set out to adopt a catalogue of international human rights.

The negotiations concluded with the adoption of the Universal Declaration of Human Rights (UDHR) in 1948. Article 19 stipulates that:

> Everyone has the right to freedom of opinion and expression; this right includes freedom to hold opinions without interference and to seek, receive and impart information and ideas through any media and regardless of frontiers.

But the road to this landmark achievement was not without friction and profound ideological disputes as Cold War tensions increased. The drafting process that led to Article 19 triggered a vehement debate on the limits of tolerance (Morsink 1999; Farrior 1996; Mchangama 2011). To what extent should Nazis and fascists be allowed to advocate the very ideologies that had covered Europe in totalitarian darkness? The foremost champions of not only permitting states to *prohibit* hate speech but making it a *duty* for all states to do so were the communist states led by the Soviet Union. The Soviet delegation argued that Article 19 could not stand alone since 'the freedom this article would give to the Nazis would undercut and threaten ... the very right affirmed in the article; without the limiting clause, the article would be self-destructive'. Most tellingly – and perhaps most decisively for the final outcome – the Soviets pushed for a phrase explicitly criminalising 'fascism' (Morsink 1999: 66–68).

American diplomats warned against any free speech restrictions which might justify authoritarian censorship norms. A number of European states were less principled than the US but thought it a step too far to include an obligation to prohibit hate speech in an international human rights declaration. These concerns ultimately defeated the Soviet proposal.

But when the UN set out to adopt the legally binding International Covenant on Civil and Political Rights (ICCPR) the conflict flared up again. In one of the first meetings, a Soviet diplomat argued that a duty to prohibit hate speech was necessary since '[m]illions had perished because the propaganda of racial and national superiority, hatred, and contempt, had not been stopped in time'.[12]

The US representative Eleanor Roosevelt emerged as a dogged defender of free speech. She warned against the Soviet proposal as 'extremely dangerous' since it:

> would only encourage Governments to punish all criticisms in the name of protection against religious or national hostility. ... [and] be exploited by totalitarian

---

12 U.N. Commission on Human Rights, 5th Sess., U.N. Doc E/CN.4/SR.123, 14 June 1949: 4 (http://hr-travaux.law.virginia.edu/document/iccpr/ecn4sr 123/nid-1820).

States for the purpose of rendering the other articles null and void.[13]

But this time around principled warnings failed to carry the day. Sixteen countries from Latin America, Africa, the Middle East and Eastern Europe proposed a text which became ICCPR Article 20(2): 'Any advocacy of national, racial or religious hatred that constitutes incitement to discrimination, hostility or violence shall be prohibited by law.' When put to a vote in the General Assembly, it was adopted with 52 votes in favour, 19 against and 12 abstentions. The 19 countries that voted against included almost all Western liberal democracies (Mchangama 2011).

Unfortunately, the concerns of Eleanor Roosevelt turned out to be prescient, as communist states used the nebulous concept of 'incitement to hatred' to punish hundreds of dissidents, human rights activists and religious believers who challenged communist rule.

Concerned about Western radio stations broadcasting uncensored news – including banned writings of dissidents – into millions of homes behind the Iron Curtain, the Soviet Union warned that it would never tolerate 'the dissemination of ... racism, fascism ... hostility among peoples and false slanderous propaganda' (Morgan 2018: 179).

Yugoslavia actively supported the Soviet line on ICCPR Article 20 at the UN while at home it criminalised incitement to hatred with punishments of up to ten years in prison. But

---

13 U.N. International Covenant on Civil and Political Rights (ICCPR), 6th Sess., U.N. Doc E/CN.4/SR.174, 28 April 1950 (http://hr-travaux.law.virginia.edu/document/iccpr/ecn4sr174/nid-1741).

this provision was used to curb political criticism as well as the religious and nationalist sentiments of the country's different ethnic groups. In 1981 an imam was sentenced to four years' imprisonment for provoking national and religious hatred after criticising the authorities and urging parents to raise their children as Muslims. An Orthodox priest and three other men were given sentences of four to six years for singing nationalist songs at a christening. The liberal Croatian writer and dissident Vlado Gotovac – sometimes called 'the Croat Vaclav Havel' – got two years for hostile propaganda and incitement to national hatred for interviews with foreign journalists (Kolb 1982).

Whereas communist states used (and abused) human rights–related exceptions to free speech to silence and punish dissidents, the dissidents themselves appealed to the core protection of free speech in international human rights law. The very first paragraph of the famous Charter 77, co-authored by Vaclav Havel, complained that '[t]he right to freedom of expression ... guaranteed by [ICCPR] Article 19 ... is in our case purely illusory'.[14]

The use of human rights language and in particular the emphasis on the robust protection of free expression created a positive feedback loop allowing dissidents to challenge censorship and oppression through the amplification of Western governments, media and human rights organisations. According to several historians, this pressure contributed to the demise of communist rule and the

---

14 Charter 77 (1 January 1977), trans. at Roy Rosenzweig Center for History and New Media (https://chnm.gmu.edu/1989/archive/files/declaration-of -charter-77_4346bae392.pdf).

mostly peaceful transition to democracy in many former communist states (Thomas 2001; Morgan 2018).

The end of the Cold War did not neutralise the potential abuse of ICCPR Article 20(2) identified by Eleanor Roosevelt in 1950. In 1999, the Organization of Islamic Cooperation (OIC) launched a more than decade-long campaign at the UN to counter 'defamation of religions'. This was an attempt to prohibit blasphemy, in particular criticism and mockery of Islam – which is banned in most of the 57 OIC member states, some of whom even prescribe the death penalty. Often these laws are targeted at religious minorities, unorthodox Muslims and secularists (Fiss and Kestenbaum 2017). Prominent victims include the Saudi blogger Raif Badawi, sentenced to ten years in prison and 1,000 lashes for secular writings on his blog. With defamation of religion the OIC sought to fuse and expand the categories of blasphemy and hate speech by incorporating the former into the latter and then use this piece of legal creationism as the platform for a free-standing prohibition on blasphemy under international law.

A typical example of a resolution on defamation of religion would urge states:

> to prohibit the dissemination, including through political institutions and organizations, of racist and xenophobic ideas and material aimed at any religion or its followers that constitute incitement to racial and religious hatred, hostility or violence.[15]

---

15 U.N. Human Rights Council resolution 7/19, Combating defamation of religions, 27 March 2008 (https://ap.ohchr.org/documents/E/HRC/resolu tions/A_HRC_RES_7_19.pdf).

In 2011 the annual OIC resolutions on defamation of religion were defeated by a US-led UN resolution.[16] It condemned advocacy of incitement to hatred, but only called on criminalising 'incitement to *imminent violence* based on religion or belief' (emphasis added). This was a standard inspired by the US Supreme Court's decision in *Brandenburg v. Ohio*, 395 U.S. 444 (1969), which held that speech could only be banned if it constituted incitement to imminent lawless action and was likely to result in such action. This invalidated an Ohio law used to convict a Ku Klux Klan leader who had denounced 'niggers' and 'Jews'. It might seem ironic that a Supreme Court case protecting the free speech of white supremacists should help defeat an attempt to legitimise the suppression of dissent in authoritarian states.

But the progressive potential of protecting the free speech of bigots would not have surprised one of the justices who joined the majority decision in Brandenburg. In 1967 Thurgood Marshall became the first African-American Supreme Court Justice. Central to Marshall's philosophy, in the words of one biographer, was the idea that 'liberty and equality, properly understood, complemented each other'. Specifically, Marshall's record of protecting free speech claims from the bench underlined his belief that (Adelman 2013: 129):

---

16 U.N. Human Rights Council resolution 16/18, Combating intolerance, negative stereotyping and stigmatization of, and discrimination, incitement to violence and violence against, persons based on religion or belief, 12 April 2011 (https://www2.ohchr.org/english/bodies/hrcouncil/docs/16session/A.HRC.RES.16.18_en.pdf).

The First Amendment also promoted equality and social justice because it afforded members of subordinated groups, whose voices are most likely to be suppressed, an opportunity to give voice to their concerns.

The continuing importance of free speech in protecting minorities

I hope this short historical sketch of past free speech struggles will serve to vindicate Thurgood Marshall's belief in the 'intersectionality' – properly understood – of free speech and equality. Because, as we have seen, there is an intimate relationship between censorship and political systems built on the subjugation of one or more groups of people whether based on race (slavery, colonialism and apartheid), political ideology (communism) or religion (Islamic blasphemy bans). In such systems restrictions on free speech – even when formally neutral – will tend to perpetuate and entrench the values of the dominant in-group and marginalise the out-group. Far from imperilling vulnerable minorities, free speech is one of their most important safeguards. It is no coincidence that Frederick Douglass, Gandhi, Martin Luther King, Nelson Mandela, and Vaclav Havel all invoked the transformative, equalising, universalist, and liberating potential of free speech in their fight to mobilise public opinion against injustice.

No doubt contemporary hate speech bans in mature and consolidated liberal democracies are more benign than the laws of the antebellum South or communist bloc. But the examples of hate speech laws targeting political, religious, artistic and symbolic speech on burning issues dividing opinion among citizens in democracies are many (Strossen 2018). And as new political orthodoxies arise, speech restrictions tend to mushroom as a result of 'scope creep' and new and unpopular minorities risk becoming the target of hate speech laws. In Germany the prohibition against the burning of flags was recently expanded with the argument that the sole aim of flag burning is to 'stir up hatred, anger and aggression', although flag-burning has often been used as a symbolic protest against government policies, such as warfare and oppression.[17] In France hate speech laws also overlap with criticism of governments and several people – many of them Muslims – have been punished for advocating a boycott of Israel.[18]

Moreover, as Eleanor Roosevelt foresaw, even with the best intentions, hate speech laws are liable to be abused by authoritarians. A year after the adoption of Germany's Network Enforcement Act thirteen countries had copy-pasted the German initiative. Among them were Russia, Belarus and Venezuela.[19] Turkey provides a particularly tragic example of how speech restrictions adopted to shield minorities can become a weapon pointed in their direction. In

---

17 Germany makes burning foreign flags a jailable offense. Deutsche Welle, 15 May 2020 (https://www.dw.com/en/germany-makes-burning-foreign-flags-a-jailable-offense/a-53445868).

18 France's criminalisation of Israel boycotts sparks free-speech debate. France 24, 21 January 2016 (https://www.france24.com/en/20160120-france-boycott-israel-bds-law-free-speech-antisemitism).

19 Germany's online crackdowns inspire the world's dictators. *Foreign Policy*, 6 November 2019 (https://foreignpolicy.com/2019/11/06/germany-online-crackdowns-inspired-the-worlds-dictators-russia-venezuela-india/).

2020 the Ankara Bar Association filed a police complaint against Turkey's Religious Affairs Directorate for provoking 'hatred and hostility' after homophobic comments by a prominent imam. As a response a prosecutor opened an investigation into the Ankara Bar Association for 'insulting ... religious values', a move supported by the Turkish Ministry of Justice.[20]

A robust and principled commitment to free speech will not defeat racism and bigotry on its own. But it does provide the victims of hatred and discrimination a platform from which to expose the bigots, appeal to common values, and deny bigoted majorities the means to impose their intolerance. Laws against hate speech, on the other hand, chart a dangerous course for the minorities they are intended to protect.

---

20 Turkey: criminal case for opposing homophobic speech. Human Rights Watch, 1 May 2020 (https://www.hrw.org/news/2020/05/01/turkey-criminal-case-opposing-homophobic-speech).

3 TOLERATING EXTREME SPEECH

Nick Cowen

How should free societies deal with people who profess support for the use of unlawful violence to achieve political ends? This is a very timely question in view of recent events. I believe that what tends to be called extreme speech should not be subject to any additional legal restrictions beyond the ordinary legal constraints on criminal activity. Police and lawmakers should focus on preventing active conspiracies to commit violence against persons and property rather than identifying extreme speech for prosecution.

My argument is as follows. Violent rhetoric is a common part of political discourse. 'Lawful' violence itself is a core feature of the way all states maintain social order. People disagree a great deal about how violence may legitimately be used and for what ends. So advocating the use of violence as a matter of policy or morality, rather than against specific individuals, cannot plausibly be considered extreme. It is hard to distinguish extreme political positions from mainstream political positions expressed in slightly different terms or from actors in different social positions. Any legal restrictions would be unevenly, and probably arbitrarily, enforced.

Fortunately, somewhat counter-intuitively, liberal democratic societies do not require the general public to agree on a shared set of fundamental values or constitutional commitments in order to function effectively. Hence, extreme views expressed in the public sphere are not a significant threat to constitutional democracy. Authorising state actors to police public opinion, by contrast, compromises civil liberties and can perversely become a source of regime instability itself.

Classical liberal free speech doctrine

What is the classical liberal conception of free speech? John Stuart Mill (2006: 18) summed up the position effectively and famously in *On Liberty*:

> This ... is the appropriate region of human liberty. It comprises, first, the inward domain of consciousness; demanding liberty of conscience, in the most comprehensive sense; liberty of thought and feeling; absolute freedom of opinion and sentiment on all subjects, practical or speculative, scientific, moral, or theological. The liberty of expressing and publishing opinions may seem to fall under a different principle, since it belongs to that part of the conduct of an individual which concerns other people; but, being almost of as much importance as the liberty of thought itself, and resting in great part on the same reasons, is practically inseparable from it.

This passage supports the right to hold and express personal opinions about any subject matter, as well as to publish and disseminate such opinions through willing channels and platforms without censorship or prior restraint.

Mill's approach reserves the strongest protection for private conduct: this includes forms of expression conducted alone, whether writing, drawing, watching or reading. It also covers spaces where anyone present is there entirely under their own volition. Mill adopted a fairly narrow notion of purely private conduct. He believed that if people are paid to participate in an association, then their exposure to expressive content is no longer relevantly voluntary for expressive purposes.

Nevertheless, this takes us quite far in terms of free expression because it means that people can discuss and display almost any expressive content in any assembly or association whether taking place in person or online. This applies so long as all people present are there because of their own interest rather than someone else's material inducement. This illustrates the value of private property, as well as proprietary communal governance for facilitating free expression. Setting clear boundaries is what generates the safe spaces, from the back room of a pub to churches, where consensual exchanges of expressive content of all kinds can take place (Cowen 2016).

Expression in public spaces is necessarily subject to greater regulation than expression taking place within the entirely voluntary private sphere. Everyone has access to, and may have to use, public space. This implies that people expressing themselves in public may not have an exclusively voluntary audience. Some restrictions on the place and manner of expression is inevitable. This includes censorship of some content held by members of the public to be offensive, threatening, provocative or obscene. Conduct perfectly appropriate in specialised settings, whether an invitation-only conference, an art gallery, or (these days especially) a password-protected video meeting, might not be appropriate for a town square or a station platform. Social media platforms such as Twitter and Facebook present some additional complications because of their sheer scale and speed of expressive interactions. Nevertheless, because they are privately governed, face competition, and offer facilities for participants blocking and muting individuals, they are probably best considered to be private settings for most purposes.

So far, this outline has focused on the content of expression. But many forms of expression can constitute social acts rather than simple descriptions or ideas (Austin 1962). Contemporary scholars now often make distinctions between the propositional content of an expression and the speech acts associated with the expression. In some contexts, what is said in terms of content can be quite different from the intentions and effects in the context in which it is expressed. For example, within criminal organisations, a boss might use a harmless-sounding speech act to commission an act of violence in a way that leaves plausible deniability.

For a few scholars, these complexities render any fundamental claims to a right to free speech hopeless and confused (Fish 1994; McGlynn and Ward 2009). The classical liberal approach instead acknowledges the challenge but still observes great social value in establishing as broad a range of free expression as possible. It rules out nearly all constraints based on judgement of the content of an expression and insists on a fairly narrow set of speech acts that attract legal sanction (Weinstein 2009). This includes direct threats of violence, inducement to commit crime as well as harassment, fraud, deception, defamation and breach of confidence or privacy.

Mill's justification for this position is that ultimately it is only through debate, discussion and disagreement that better ideas for improving our personal and social lives, as well as public affairs, can become established (Waldron 1987). Mill's Whiggish optimism that the best ideas will win out if only all barriers to their expression were lifted has, though, been tempered by historical experience. Public discussion and promulgation of competing doctrines do not necessarily lead to continuous improvement in the quality of public opinion. Nevertheless, it is still widely recognised among liberals that freedom of expression and robust debate are essential for holding governments to account and respecting people's rights to pursue their own plans in their own way.

Is extremism exceptional?

I have outlined a classical liberal free speech jurisprudence, including a number of ways that expression can be legitimately limited. The question at hand is whether some forms of speech might not be covered under these generally legitimate constraints but nevertheless require restriction. Are there some sorts of utterances that merely by their content, not their intent or effect, require restriction?

This is a vexed question throughout the history of liberal thought. John Locke famously supported religious toleration and freedom of association but excluded Catholics and atheists from sharing these rights. Locke's reasoning was that Catholic doctrine stood in direct opposition to the religious liberty of Protestants and an independent English state. Atheists were excluded because they were supposedly unable to take oaths or make covenants, and so could not participate effectively in the institutions of civil society. It is not entirely clear whether Locke saw Catholic doctrine as intrinsically incompatible with English liberty, or something more historically contingent and potentially fixable.[1] Although hostility to Catholicism may seem absurd today, there are parallel arguments and discussions (even among a few self-professed liberals) as to whether Islamist-inspired terrorism is ultimately sanctioned by Islamic theology. A historically informed outlook suggests that such links between broader ideology and violence are highly contingent.

Reflecting twentieth-century experience with Nazism and authoritarian communism, Karl Popper (1945) offered a more secular and abstract rendition of the problem that he called 'the paradox of tolerance'. Popper argued that limitless tolerance would be self-defeating for liberal societies, as intolerant groups would exploit their civic freedom

---

1 Locke was subject to a number of speech restrictions himself so he may have been unable to push his case for toleration to a logical conclusion.

to gain power but would then deny others the freedom to contest their ideas. The bar he set for legitimacy was high: the willingness of extremists to engage in rational argument to defend their views. The common theme is the concern that certain sorts of professed beliefs are not only mistaken but have the capacity over the long run to undermine a regime. Hence, today we tend to identify extremists as people opposed to democracy and human rights, the current public justification for broadly liberal regimes.

Contemporary scholars who favour speech restrictions focus on hateful beliefs surrounding identity and group characteristics such as gender, race, ethnicity and religion (Langton 2009; Waldron 2012). Hate speech, especially against vulnerable minorities, is widely perceived to exist along a continuum of action that leads to threats and actual violence.

More broadly, such expression diminishes the social status of groups in need of protection. In making these arguments, scholars normally target a supposed 'free speech principle' that conceives proponents of free speech as supporting it regardless of the consequences or denying the possibility of major consequences of hate speech. Such principled proponents of free speech have made their case in the past (Dworkin 2013). But my approach is more practical. It is important to recognise social harms associated with hate speech. We have moral duties to oppose actions that harm people, especially the vulnerable (Howard 2019).

Nevertheless, these moral duties are better enforced through voluntary means (Bejan 2017). Attempting to introduce legal restrictions will not work practically because hatred is a ubiquitous human emotion that naturally appears in political contexts as well. The violent results of some forms of hatred must be contained but trying to eliminate it as a root cause will be self-undermining. My defence of free speech is political rather than moral (Zivi 2012).

Everyday extremism

The key problem for proponents of speech regulation aimed only at extremists is that looking too carefully at people's beliefs suggests a great many of them lack even minimal loyalty to liberal ideals. Democracy itself receives only tepid support (Foa and Mounk 2017). Classical liberals tend to be aware that adherents to their system of thought (for example, commitment to free trade and immigration without borders, and the decriminalisation of all drugs and sex work) are a tiny minority of the population. More mainstream liberals, by contrast, are inclined to imagine that there is an overlapping consensus about what constitutes the range of reasonable views. This is not the case, at least if systematic surveys are to be believed. What we might consider to be extremist beliefs turn out to be widely held. Current anti-extremist policies tend to focus on 'far-right' racist movements and Islamic extremism. But in both these cases, making a division between extremists and mainstream adherents of a socio-political discourse is fraught with difficulties.

A substantial minority of the British public self-identifies as racist in surveys (Meadowcroft 2020).[2] At the same

---

2   This will not surprise members of any visible ethnic minority.

time, Islamist beliefs are not uncommon among Muslims. A majority of Muslims believe that homosexuality should be criminalised and a substantial minority support the imposition of Sharia law.[3] Nevertheless, a majority of Muslims feel a strong sense of British national belonging. This is in no way a contradiction. As with white racists, holding irrational, potentially violent, prejudices against minority groups is common in Britain and apparently in every society – including among minority groups themselves. Although some individuals are more intolerant against difference than others, some degree of intolerance is common. Principled tolerance is seldom observed within individuals or groups even if the regime is relatively tolerant.

Violent political discourse is not limited to far-right groups. For example, anarchists under the banner of Class War commonly participate in mainstream UK public protests on the left. They are known for deploying graphic imagery, for example of the heads of conservative leaders being sliced by axes. Online activists taunt each other with violent cartoons and images. Alt-right online activists show people dangling out of helicopters in reference to assassination techniques deployed in Chile in the 1980s while communists display images of guillotines in affirmation of the French Revolution. This should not surprise, as what political activists are doing is contesting the legitimate use of force within societies that often respond to social

3   C4 survey and documentary reveals What British Muslims Really Think. Channel 4, 11 April 2016 (https://www.channel4.com/press/news/c4-sur vey-and-documentary-reveals-what-british-muslims-really-think).

problems with the use of violence. For example, we can imagine a scenario where the idea that the state should imprison people for selling cannabis or failing to pay council tax is considered extreme, perhaps as peripheral an idea as banning people from wearing odd socks in public. Yet cannabis prohibition and imprisonment for non-payment of council taxes are currently state policy. What is considered extreme does not emerge from a systematic principle, but from the contingences of the status quo.

The fact that 'extremism' is so widespread can lead to the mischaracterisation of merely unpopular positions as extreme. For example, a recent cross-party anti-extremism campaign identified pro-republican Labour Party members as extremist (Mainstream 2019). The monarchy is popular in this country, and converting the United Kingdom into a republic hardly seems likely to resolve any pressing public policy problems, so campaigners tend to be ignored. Nevertheless, the most cursory glance at Britain's allies reveals plenty of examples of republican governments that perform as well as constitutional monarchies. Campaigning for such a regime in the UK (non-violently) can hardly constitute extremism even on the generous definitions that some anti-extremist campaigners use.

This difficulty with differentiating the content of extreme positions from mainstream positions has troubling implications for the way most anti-extremist policy is conceptualised. Refusing to tolerate the intolerant as a matter of state policy would imply either one or both of these approaches:

- systematically excluding a large minority of the population from basic freedoms to express their views and participate in political life;
- selectively targeting people who hold anti-democratic views and are considered particularly dangerous to the regime or prone to turning to violence.

Both these approaches tend to undermine the very liberal commitments that they are supposed to protect. For example, Greece introduced tests of national loyalty during the Cold War in order to combat a threat of communist insurgency. As a result, people considered to be communist sympathisers were excluded from positions of public authority and much of economic life. This undermined civil liberties for generations, slowing Greece's transition towards stable democracy, and contributed to an emerging scheme of clientelist control over the wider economy (Trantidis 2016). The ubiquity of hatred between groups in civil society presents various social problems but allowing it to drive state policy as well generates an active danger.

Recent analyses of the British government's official anti-extremism 'Prevent' programme are illustrative of the second approach (Skoczylis 2015; Skoczylis and Andrews 2019). As the name suggests, it is an attempt to broaden standard anti-terrorism policy to include individuals considered at risk of joining extremist groups. These individuals are often identified by the type of views they espouse and the literature and online media they access, that are said to be opposed to British values. An intractable problem for people implementing this policy has been defining what contravenes British values in a way that does not stereotype minorities. This easily leads to already marginalised individuals feeling deliberately stigmatised and demonised. Moreover, Prevent creates public duties for officials unrelated to state security (including teachers and academics) to report on the views of their service users. It makes everyone a participant in state surveillance. Such a policy, fortunately only implemented on a relatively small scale so far, is a case of unintentionally undermining liberal values in the very attempt to protect them.

A taste for violence

If holding hateful, prejudicial, anti-democratic views is insufficient to mark individuals as a small minority in the general population, what explains the minority who join the active groups that concern anti-extremist policy? This is still a live question in academic research. Nevertheless, Meadowcroft and Morrow (2017) offer some promising insights. They explore this puzzle through the lens of the logic of collective action. Focusing on far-right groups, and especially the English Defence League (EDL), they explain that different kinds of participants join such movements for various reasons. The majority of EDL participants have relatively little social capital and self-esteem but enjoy participating in violence. This is why many EDL supporters were recruited from the ranks of football hooligans. The organisation offered them regular opportunities to engage in violence alongside a sense of visceral solidarity against a perceived enemy.

Founders of extremist groups have a higher tolerance for working alone or in smaller groups. They are prepared to accept, and perhaps even enjoy, the stigma associated with public infamy. What is their motivation? Rather than merely holding common violent prejudices, their belief systems are much more distinctive and atypical than those of the general population. They normally develop them early in life. Their views are often complex, conspiratorial and mystical, characterised by peculiar beliefs about the way that human society operates. In the West, founders are more likely to have an obsessive hatred of Jews over and above visible ethnic minorities, curiously a characteristic of both Western white supremacists and Islamists (Meadowcroft 2020).

These beliefs are controversial and easily characterised as deviant when exposed in public. They are not a point of attraction for most members of violent political groups. If discussed openly, they could undermine support for a movement's leadership. As a result, founders sometimes adopt esoteric strategies when attempting to build political movements. A mainstream political view that is hard to differentiate from ordinary political party platforms (but more aggressively and simply presented) is disseminated to aid recruitment, while a loyal, intellectually committed cadre is taught the 'real' aims of the group. On the far left, the esoteric revolutionary Socialist Workers Party adopted and manipulated mainstream anti-war positions in order to aid party recruitment (Thomas 2003). There is also some evidence that the far right attempted to exploit minority but widespread opposition to the lockdown in response to the Covid-19 pandemic.[4]

The life course and psychology of leaders of extremist movements suggest it is unlikely that censorship can prevent their emergence. There is enough in 'mainstream' political writings and philosophy to develop a sophisticated intellectual mindset that justifies violence. At the same time, it is not mainly ideology that extremists use to support wider recruitment. So specific speech restrictions are not generally helpful in depriving leaders of the resources they use to become powerful. On the other hand, it is possible that free speech restrictions aimed at combating extremism could unwittingly aid the strategy of esotericism. If there is a widespread sense that 'you can't talk about this' then that can provide cover for silences and logical gaps in a discourse. Clever leaders can use strategies such as edgy humour and irony to hide real intellectual differences that are actually vast within an extremist movement's organisation.

Alternatives to restrictions on speech content

If attempts to censor extremist speech are unlikely to be effective, what should policymakers do instead? First, we need some perspective. The fact that highly anti-social beliefs and preferences persist in the general public is

---

4   Police vow to break up planned anti-lockdown protests in UK cities. *The Guardian*, 14 May 2020 (https://www.theguardian.com/uk-news/2020/may/14/police-vow-to-break-up-planned-anti-lockdown-protests-in-uk-cities).

evidence that liberal democracy does not require faithful adherence to its basic values in order to function (Cowen 2018). A plausible alternative explanation is that most people hold their political beliefs quite lightly. Values are not a strong motivation for action compared to more ordinary commitments to personal wellbeing and obligations to family, friends, co-workers and the local community.

Moreover, most people fear and avoid violence. Therefore, any political system which maintains social order and credibly signals its capability to provide security is unlikely to face serious domestic threats from the general population. Hateful and extremist beliefs only motivate widespread violent action against a regime when people feel physically insecure or their material wellbeing is seriously threatened. As a result, people concerned about democratic stability should pay more attention to the strategies and institutional constraints of elite political actors rather than 'extremists' who are almost inevitably peripheral (Trantidis and Cowen 2020). Ideological and civil pluralism, alongside checks and balances that political actors are incentivised to defend, is a surer mechanism for maintaining liberal institutions compared to seeking ideological purity (Cowen 2018; Trantidis 2017).

What about dealing with the minority of activists associated with explicitly violent extremist groups? Their taste for violence makes them a genuine threat to public order and this could eventually lead to political instability. But because most people joining violent groups are only vaguely motivated by ideology, they cannot be defeated ideologically. A more promising approach is to restrict the capabilities of leaders of extremist groups to supply violent experiences to their activists.

Morrow and Meadowcroft (2019) conclude that the English Defence League lost strength as a political force partly because of internal contradictions associated with attempts to scale up the organisation, but also because police adopted a strategy of 'kettling' supporters during street protests.[5] The EDL were allowed to protest but were isolated from counter-protestors and prevented from coming and going as they pleased. They were kept to a specific place or route. Essentially, police made EDL protests a boring and uncomfortable experience for participants, rather than exciting and empowering. Since most participants were seeking an exciting experience rather than political power, denying the experience through this channel was effective at reducing recruitment and participation.

Besides violent protests that tend to attract attention, there are also many everyday threats of violence and harassment against visible ethnic minorities (Awan and Zempi 2016; Zempi 2017). As discussed above, harassment in public settings or expressions made to non-consenting individuals are not covered under free speech protections. Both criminal law and civil remedies are appropriate for tackling violence of this kind. This would be a better use of police resources.

---

5   Kettling involves large cordons of police officers moving to corral a crowd within a limited area for extended periods.

Conclusion

In this chapter, I have outlined the classical liberal approach to free speech and explored the case for treating political extremism as an exception to strong protection of freedom of speech. I have suggested that holding potentially violent prejudices and anti-democratic sentiments is more common than imagined in liberal democracies. This confounds policies that attempt to select people expressing extremist sentiments for sanctions or other forms of intervention aiming at their reform. It also contradicts liberal democratic values. A more promising approach lies in attempts within civil society to foster tolerance and respect for differences (Bejan 2017).

I have pointed out that many people attracted to violent extremism are not particularly ideologically driven but are more interested in physical confrontations. The core leadership of extremist movements tries to attract recruits by offering access to group-sanctioned violence, as well as a sense of social mission and solidarity which their followers struggle to obtain in other parts of their lives. Depriving extremist leaders of the capacity to supply violence is likely to be more successful, alongside proactive attempts to prevent violence and harassment against minorities. Supplying less dangerous sources of solidarity and meaning for people attracted to extremism would be a useful long-term solution. State censorship of extreme views, however, is both illiberal and unlikely to be effective.

4 LEGISLATION ON ONLINE HARMS WILL DAMAGE FREE SPEECH

Victoria Hewson

Communication of ideas and information is now overwhelmingly done electronically, whether user-generated or editorial, publicly shared on social media or privately shared by direct messages or file sharing. The reach and decentralised nature of online communications have long worried governments, concerned about terrorists, child abusers and other criminals using the Internet to plot and execute their activities. There have been legal battles, as security services sought access to private communications and data through surveillance and data retention obligations on service providers, resisted by civil liberties groups and liberty-minded politicians.

Despite this, in the Western world at least, online communications, especially social media, seemed to showcase classical liberal values of toleration, limited government and voluntary association. Free speech and (virtual) assembly flourished and opinions could be expressed in groups or to the world at large, subject only to the bounds of the general law and the conduct rules of the platform, unrestricted by state-sanctioned views of decency or suitability. As we will see in this chapter, this situation is increasingly under threat, especially in the EU and the UK, as governments exercise increasing control over what is communicated online. They purport to adhere to liberal principles, by justifying measures in terms of harm prevention. But by defining harm to include being misled, distressed or offended, they are in danger of restricting the private sphere and free markets with little supporting evidence, doubtful prospects of success in countering genuinely harmful activity, and great risk of unintended consequences.

Measures have been pursued by EU institutions, Parliamentary committees, government departments, charities, academics and media campaigns. The breadth of the types of harms they wish to counter and of content that they wish to regulate is staggering. Disinformation, hate speech, electoral manipulation, microtargeting, trolling, bullying, offensive speech, child abuse, self-harm, terrorism, cybercrime, poor sleep quality, harassment – governments want to protect us from all of these, and they have decided to enlist intermediaries to do it for them. These moves towards both regulating content and outsourcing responsibility for enforcement on to private providers are troubling and seem in many ways to be driven by a moral panic.

This chapter focuses on two measures in particular: the UK government's Online Harms White Paper, and the EU's Code of Practice on Disinformation. It goes on to consider how these developments affect, or are affected by, the established protections from liability for Internet intermediaries, and the relationship between free markets and free speech online.

Legal but harmful

In the UK there are many laws and regulations that govern the lawfulness of speech – laws of defamation, negligence, malicious communications, laws relating to harassment, terrorism, child sexual exploitation. Some of these laws are investigated and enforced proactively by the authorities, to prevent publication of terrorist and extremist material, for example, and there have been growing efforts to harness the power of Internet intermediaries as gatekeepers to identify and suppress illegal material at source.

Despite persistent rhetoric about the online world as a 'Wild West' of lawlessness,[1] a 2018 review by the Law Commission found that criminal laws apply equally, possibly more stringently, in the online world as offline. But there are differences, both legal and practical, between how these laws apply in the online and offline worlds. In legal terms, under a longstanding EU law (Article 14 of the e-Commerce Directive[2]) Internet platforms are not liable for unlawful content that they host, unless they fail to remove it promptly when they are aware, or should have been aware, of it.[3] They also cannot be required to monitor proactively content posted by users, under Article 15

---

1 For example, then Secretary of State for Digital, Culture, Media and Sport, Matt Hancock, declared in 2018 that 'the Wild West for tech companies is over' (https://www.telegraph.co.uk/technology/2018/03/18/wild-west-era-technology-firms-like-facebook-google-minister/).

2 Directive 2000/31/EC, at the time of writing still applicable in the UK, and, in principle to be carried into UK law after the end of the Transition Period.

3 Under the equivalent law in the US, the so-called 'notice and take down' qualification does not apply. Under s.230 of the Communications Decency

of the same directive. This distinguishes hosts of online content from publishers and creators. If platforms fail to remove content that they know about, they can be subject to criminal prosecution or civil action, which of course they can defend in the normal way and will eventually only be liable if a court finds against them. In such cases all normal protections in law for freedom of expression and public interest apply. The outlook for this legal framework is considered further below.

In practical terms, however, the volume of content that is hosted and shared online, the relative absence of geographical or jurisdictional barriers to its dissemination and the possibility for anonymity, make general laws harder to enforce in the digital realm. There is a perception that these factors enable the commission of crimes and have caused an increase in offences such as terrorism and child abuse.

The proliferation of digital interactions beyond simply sharing static content into fast-moving interactive forums such as Twitter, and entertainment apps, has given rise to the UK government's concerns about wellbeing, especially that of children. The government has already used the vehicle of data protection law to empower the Information Commissioner to produce a Code of Practice on Age Appropriate Design[4] that will impose a duty on all operators

---

Act, platforms' immunity, other than in respect of copyright violations and federal criminal matters, is absolute.

4   https://ico.org.uk/for-organisations/guide-to-data-protection/key-data
-protection-themes/age-appropriate-design-a-code-of-practice-for-online
-services/#:~:text=The%20code%20is%20a%20set,designing%20and%20
developing%20online%20services

of websites to act in the best interests of any child who may access their site. This means they must either make their site suitable for children or implement formal age controls to prevent children from accessing it. If they do not do so, the Information Commissioner may consider them to be in violation of data protection laws, with all the financial sanctions and reputational damage which this entails.

The Home Office and Department for Digital, Culture, Media and Sport (DCMS) have gone further, and wish to appoint a regulator, and platforms acting under codes of practice, as overseers of the personal wellbeing of adults and children. In 2019 the Government published the Online Harms White Paper. In 2020 it published a response to the White Paper consultation and a final policy position. A draft 'Online Safety Bill' is expected in the course of 2021. The White Paper set out a regulatory framework to counter 'Illegal and unacceptable content and activity': from terrorist plots and radicalisation to children's mental health and wellbeing; from child sexual abuse to 'echo chambers' and 'filter bubbles'; from gang culture to excessive screen time.

The framework will apply to 'companies that allow users to share or discover user-generated content or interact with each other online ... including social media platforms, file hosting sites, public discussion forums, messaging services and search engines'. Service providers will be under a statutory duty of care 'overseen and enforced by an independent regulator'. The duty of care, as refined after the consultation, will be to 'improve safety for users of online services, and to prevent other people from being harmed as a direct consequence of content or activity on those services' (Department for Culture, Media and Sport and Home Office 2020). While the White Paper provided examples of harm, such as bullying and undermining civil discourse, a definition of harm, or unacceptability, was deliberately omitted. The consultation response, however, conceded that 'a general definition of harmful content and activity' would be provided, with 'priority categories' of harm to be set out in secondary legislation. It also appeared to limit the scope of 'harmful content' to only that which 'gives rise to a reasonably foreseeable risk of a significant adverse physical or psychological impact on individuals'. While this seems to be an improvement on the original proposal, misinformation and disinformation are still considered to be in-scope harms, and content that is legal will still be subject to the duty of care.

The use of the expression 'duty of care' in the White Paper bears little resemblance to the concept as it currently exists in law. There is no precedent for such a general duty of care to prevent third parties from doing harm to each other. Creating a legal duty of care, whereby a platform could be held liable for actual damage suffered by individuals because of its actions or inaction would at least be legally consistent, but of course this is not the intention of the Government. Proving loss or damage as a result of a breach of duty of care owed by a platform to a user is in reality likely to be impossible and would not capture all of the harms in the Government's sights, or all of the people it wishes to protect.

As noted by leading lawyer Graham Smith in his response to the Online Harms Consultation, the creation of such a new type of duty will create a parallel legal system for online and offline content. It is likely to result in suppression of material that the UK Supreme Court has held[5] should be not be suppressed, even if it would be distressing to a child reading it. It would also undermine the repeal of blasphemy laws (Smith 2020):

> The White Paper proposals would enable the regulator to deem blasphemous material to be harmful and to require intermediaries, as part of their duty of care, to take steps to restrict or, possibly, suppress it. Thus, by a sidewind, a deliberate decision of Parliament would be circumvented.

In practice this would mean that content that is legal in a book or newspaper could violate a regulator's code of practice against harmful material online. The online platform would be obliged to remove it or block it from being shared in the first place, but a book or newspaper publisher would not be restricted from publishing it.

Generations of lawmakers and judges have made and applied laws in ways that have sought to balance protecting lives, property and reputations against protecting free expression. This has not always been perfectly achieved and there are many laws that arguably infringe unduly on free speech.[6] Even then, perpetrators will have the right to

---

5   In *Rhodes v OPO* [2015] UKSC 32.

6   For example, sending a communication that is indecent or grossly offensive is an offence under the Malicious Communications Act; displaying

defend themselves, evidentiary standards must be reached and prosecutors will take public interest considerations into account. Technology companies removing content at source by automated means, in order to protect themselves from censure by a regulator, will never be able to reflect this balance of interests.

While they contained assertions and assurances about free speech safeguards, the White Paper and the DCMS/Home Office response showed little sign that these vital legal points have been taken into account.

The enforcement powers proposed for the regulator included issuing fines and blocking access to non-compliant websites and apps. The possibility of personal liability for individuals is being held in reserve.

Which body can be expected to safeguard free speech and regulate material shared online? The Home Office and DCMS have confirmed that Ofcom will be the regulator of online harms. Ofcom is already the regulator of broadcast media. Recently, it has controversially censured broadcasters for a presenter's comments that 'risked undermining viewers' trust in advice from public authorities' and for exposing viewers to harm by interviewing conspiracy theorist David Icke (Ofcom 2020). Scaling up the powers and resources of this regulator to police the terms and conditions of, and content and behaviour on, platforms anywhere in the world that are visible in the UK does not augur well for freedom of expression and association.

---

writing or other visible representation that is 'abusive' and likely to cause harassment, alarm or distress is an offence under the Public Order Act.

In policy terms, it is the argument of this chapter that the whole basis of the Online Harms agenda seems misplaced. There is little evidence that criminal activities are caused or exacerbated by the availability of Internet platforms; if anything the Internet has brought 'hypertransparency' to such activities. Rather than there being more harms and crimes in the world, they are more visible and this has given rise to a moral panic (Mueller 2015).

Some things that children are exposed to online, such as incitement to suicide and self-harm and sharing of sexual imagery, are horrifying and harmful, but it does not follow that intermediaries should be responsible for countering these harms. A review of evidence for the Independent Inquiry into Child Sexual Abuse (CSA) found that (Wager et al. 2018):

> the online world is safe for most young people ... Also, there is an increased familiarity with online risks and how to manage them among parents and young people. However there are gaps in the current understanding of the scale of online-facilitated CSA. There is a particular lack of evidence in relation to England and Wales, which restricts the accurate assessment of the scale of online-facilitated CSA in this country.

The Commons Science and Technology Committee considered that its 2018/19 inquiry into the impact of social media and screen use on young people's health had been 'hindered by the limited quantity and quality of academic evidence available'. It was 'surprised to find that [the Government] has not commissioned any new, substantive research to help inform its proposals [for new legislation]'.[7]

While it is difficult to prove that the prevalence of criminality and child abuse, as opposed to their visibility, has increased commensurately with the growth in online content sharing, it is in the interests of politicians and activist organisations in the field to claim causality. This justifies their claiming more power and influence over intermediaries and, indirectly, over us all. A better approach, in light of the increased visibility (which should surely assist in the investigation of such offences), would be to resource law enforcement and international efforts to investigate and punish the offenders (Aaronson et al. 2019). The Law Commission recommended reform of relevant criminal laws for clarity and effectiveness, and there may be a case for creating new criminal offences such as inciting a minor to suicide and self-harm. Sophisticated cross-border cooperation would be required for better investigation and enforcement, but this would equally be the case for enforcement of the proposed regulatory framework.

As to the prevention of nebulous categories of harm, there are good reasons why not everything that is harmful or undesirable is illegal. The state and its proxies intervening in such matters presents threats not just to freedom of expression but to the fundamentals of personal autonomy in a free society.

---

7 Undeterred by the lack of evidence, the Committee considered that something must still be done and recommended sweeping regulatory interventions.

Disinformation and fake news

In autumn 2018, the European Commission produced a Code of Practice on Disinformation.[8] It was entered into by technology companies and social media platforms, including Google, Facebook and Twitter. Disinformation was defined as:

> 'verifiably false or misleading information' which (a) 'is created, presented and disseminated for economic gain or to intentionally deceive the public'; and (b) 'may cause public harm'.
>
> 'Public harm' is in turn defined as 'threats to democratic, political and policymaking processes as well as public goods such as the protection of EU citizens' health, the environment or security'.

Somewhat hopefully, it continued:

> The notion of 'Disinformation' does not include misleading advertising, reporting errors, satire and parody, or clearly identified partisan news and commentary.

The way the Code has been applied in practice, however, shows that the idea of disinformation has been interpreted very broadly – arguably of necessity, since the volume of content that platforms have to moderate is vast and can only be overseen by automated means applying generalised rules.

---

8   Shaping Europe's digital future (europa.eu).

Signatories agreed that there need to be safeguards against disinformation and that they should 'dilute the visibility of disinformation by improving the findability of trustworthy content' and 'facilitate content discovery and access to different news sources representing alternative viewpoints', presumably whether the user wants such content and viewpoints or not. They committed to investing in 'technological means to prioritise relevant, authentic and authoritative information where appropriate in search, feeds or other automatically ranked distribution channels'.

The Code of Practice was prompted by widespread concerns (at least among establishment media and politicians) that democracies were being overrun with fake news and manipulative advertising by foreign powers and unscrupulous campaigners, leading unsuspecting, malleable viewers and readers to vote for Brexit and Donald Trump. In fact, there is little evidence that, for example, Russian bots or microtargeted campaign messaging had a defining influence on any election or vote (Bayer et al. 2017; Flynn et al. 2017). It is easier, though, for incumbent politicians to attribute the rise of populism to dark arts and manipulation (which they can then righteously seek to eliminate) than to any substantive concerns or political beliefs and values (which might require them to act to address the concerns or make the substantive case for their values). In this light, the anti-disinformation agenda pursued by the European Union, also reflected in the UK Online Harms White Paper, is troubling for both freedom of expression and the future of democracy. It also unbalances the legal regime that has so far governed the liability of intermediaries for third party content and that has allowed the digital economy to grow, as discussed further below.

Take, for example, the reliance placed by the Code of Practice on trusted fact-checkers as part of the effort to prioritise authoritative content. When subject matter may be highly contestable or unclear, a fact check will not always be useful in establishing whether content is right or wrong, misleading or harmful. Fact-checkers are not themselves free of bias – in particular when they are approved by the Government itself, as the Code of Practice envisages. This did not go unnoticed by President Trump. His fury at being 'fact-checked' by Twitter (by reference to a news organisation that is widely considered to have adopted a political position of its own) provoked executive action that opened up questions about the legal basis of platform liability in the US (and, as a result, across the world).[9] Global technology companies are being mandated to filter and censor content by the authorities in Europe, and have been threatened with punitive action in the US for doing so.

Signatories to the Code of Practice may have hoped that by enthusiastically joining in a voluntary process, they would stave off the possibility of formal regulation. If so they seem likely to be disappointed; the EU's Justice Commissioner told the European Parliament in May 2020

---

9   Executive Order on Preventing Online Censorship, 28 May 2020, seeks to 'clarify' that the immunity under section 230 should not extend to 'provide protection for those who purport to provide users a forum for free and open speech, but in reality use their power over a vital means of communication to engage in deceptive or pretextual actions stifling free and open debate by censoring certain viewpoints'.

that the experience of the Covid-19 pandemic showed the need for regulation to enable the Commission to go further in working with platforms to 'remove messages from social media'.

The impossibility of policing disinformation fairly and without prejudicing free speech was illustrated in the course of the 2020 Covid-19 outbreak. Videos carrying critical discussions of government policies were supressed by YouTube, while the BBC on occasion carried highly misleading statistics with impunity. This is not a call for the BBC to be fact-checked and down-rated for untrustworthy content; but these cases illustrate the inconsistencies and biases that are in play and the impossibility of definitively determining and pronouncing on the reliability of information. A free and open debate on contentious matters, even, or perhaps especially, difficult and technical subjects, is vital to reach the truth and for the truth to be widely believed. State-mandated suppression of conspiracy theories will not eliminate these theories but will rather lend them credibility in some eyes.

Rowing back from safe harbours

Social media platforms are private operators and therefore not bound to respect the freedom of expression of users. They are entitled to implement whatever fact-checking and moderation policies they see fit. But, as illustrated by the examples above, governments are intervening to coerce private operators into limiting free speech on their platforms. This is a reverse of the aims of the legal 'safe harbours' that have underpinned the development of the digital economy.

For twenty years the EU's e-Commerce Directive has required that service providers who merely host content will not be liable for unlawful material, unless they had knowledge of it and failed to remove it. The UK government had announced[10] an intention to review these existing liability frameworks to make them 'work better'. It appears though, according to the Online Harms White Paper, that it has decided against this, for now. The White Paper posited that new *ex ante* regulation will deliver a balance between 'existing law that enables platforms to operate' and increased responsibilities to maintain processes and governance to 'reduce the risk of illegal and harmful activity'.

Under the Directive, platforms can already be liable for content where they have gone beyond passive hosting, and there is a body of case law where this has happened. So the Online Harms framework and Code of Practice on Disinformation themselves may not transgress Article 14 of the European Convention on Human Rights directly, but they seem to mandate the platforms to act in ways that could take them outside of the immunity. Platforms risk not only being penalised by regulators for allowing 'harmful' or 'unacceptable' content to be shared, but also becoming liable under the general law as a result of their efforts to comply with regulation. All of this will have serious effects on free

---

10 In a speech by Theresa May at the World Economic Forum in Davos, January 2018.

speech online, illustrating the reasons for the liability safe harbours in the first place.[11]

It is widely believed that safe harbours were introduced around the world to nurture the development of Internet services or to prevent the inequity of liability for material outside their control. Technology companies would certainly have lobbied for and welcomed them for this reason. But the immunities from liability also brought wider social benefits. Platforms were not to be treated as creators, speakers or publishers because the liability that attaches to those roles in law would have incentivised them to remove and filter content that may be lawful, but is not worth the risk to the platform of carrying it. The interests and incentives of platforms and users diverge. Without immunity from liability for material produced by others, platforms would filter lawful content that creators themselves would be content to publish at their own risk. This 'collateral censorship' would result in the loss of content that is beneficial to society (Wu 2011). European governments today seem to believe that the benefits of free circulation and exchange of information and ideas are outweighed by the potential harmfulness, unacceptability or illegality of some of them. What had been seen as the dangers of collateral censorship are now seen as a benefit, or a tool for government to exercise control of online speech through the intermediaries.

---

11 The recitals to the Directive reference the 'free movement of information society services' as 'a specific reflection in Community law of a more general principle, namely freedom of expression as enshrined in Article 10(1) [of the ECHR]'.

Arguments for reviewing the liability safe harbours because social media platforms can and do control content that they host are seductive. Why should they benefit from (extremely valuable) protection from liability that traditional publishers do not have? But withdrawing the immunity after large platforms have benefited from it for decades, building their models without the legal and regulatory costs of liability for user content, risks entrenching the current dominant social media operators, stifling the ability of smaller and newer competitors to grow under similarly benign conditions. Retaining the favourable legal immunities but adding *ex ante* regulation seems likely to deliver a worst-of-all-worlds outcome: aggressive filtering and censorship through use of costly technologies and human resources that will create barriers to entry for new platforms and technologies, while incumbent platforms can absorb these costs and continue to enjoy the established protections from *ex post* liability.

Free speech needs free enterprise

Restrictions on free speech that will result from regulations such as those in place or being developed in the UK and EU are arguably more damaging than rules established by platforms acting autonomously. Platforms can have different policies and serve different audiences, so having individual platforms that are restrictive in their moderation does not necessarily have an adverse effect on freedom of expression. However, there could be serious adverse effects on free speech if the state intervenes to require all platforms to restrict content in furtherance of government policy, or threatens regulation such that platforms proactively do so to seem cooperative and be involved in shaping regulation to suit their interests.

Outsourcing the enforcement of restrictions to private operators will likely mean that private operators will act to restrict and filter 'harmful' content in ways that suit their commercial and private interests without accountability for policy implications. They will have to rely on automated means to do so. They will not have the incentive or the capacity to consider all the defences and mitigations that might be available in respect of a piece of content. And they will have their own political biases. It may be possible to make such private operators more transparent and open in their decision-making, and even appoint some kind of ombudsman to oversee that it is operated fairly,[12] but that would erode further the private rights of individuals to run their businesses and require yet more regulation.

Having intermediaries filter content to enforce law and policy is popular with governments and intellectual property rightsholders as it considered to be a low-cost approach to addressing content that is illegal (or simply undesirable) posted by thousands of, often unidentifiable, users. However, outsourcing compliance in this way comes with costs of its own. Illegality is hard to identify

---

12 As put forward, for example, by Professor Lilian Edwards in evidence to the House of Lords Select Committee on Regulation of the Internet and the Santa Clara Principles, published in 2018 by a group of organisations, advocates, and academic experts who support the right to free expression online.

with certainty; harmfulness and acceptability, impossible. False positives will abound. Collateral censorship and monitoring of individuals (in tension with privacy and data protection laws) will be the norm. This is already the direction of travel under instruments such as the EU Communication on Illegal Content from 2017 and the Netz-DG[13] in Germany: automated solutions are encouraged and success is judged by takedown rates, favouring volume and speed over nuance.

A fool's errand?

While the endeavour to eliminate disinformation and harm from the Internet seems likely to be a fool's errand, great damage could be done in the process. The emphasis on harm reduction 'by design' in the Online Harms White Paper and the Code of Practice on Disinformation hints at the hubris that underlies them. The idea that IT and compliance professionals simply need to apply their skills and foresight to design away harm, and that they will do so in ways that respect freedom of expression and are free from bias, under a regulator capable of monitoring the compliance of potentially every interactive platform in the world is almost laughable. It is also naive to think that the technical capabilities that platforms will deploy and the powers that governments will accrue will always be used respectfully, even in liberal democracies. Such

13 The Network Enforcement Act, which came into force in 2018, requires social media providers to remove 'obviously' illegal content within 24 hours and other illegal content within seven days or be fined up to €50 million.

regulations can be used in partisan ways: claiming that a political or philosophical opponent's words are harmful or unacceptable will be used as a tool to obstruct or silence them. Western countries used to express disapproval at censorship of the Internet by authoritarian regimes; now they seem to be suggesting it is a moral duty of the state.

The assumption by authorities that they know what is harmful or unacceptable and have a duty to protect people from it is itself authoritarian. The idea that adults need government guidance and protection to prevent them from being offended or exploited by 'purveyors of disinformation', or that governments and social media platforms are in a better position than parents to supervise screen time and content for children, is unsettling. It will be counter-productive if parents come to believe that the Internet has been made safe for children and less supervision is required. If ministers and campaigners consider that parents are not exercising enough supervision and control of children's lives online at present, the online harms framework will make that worse (potentially resulting in a cycle of ever stricter measures). Governments should surely be wary of such incursion into homes and private lives if they wish to claim to be defenders of personal responsibility and the family.

The UK and the EU are taking great risks in moving towards content regulation. Measures such as those discussed in this chapter are unlikely to reduce harm or protect democracy, but could mean losses in trust in institutions, and reductions in freedom of expression and association. There will be economic costs if innovation and competition suffer and the vast consumer surplus from digital services dissipates. Measures such as age verification and requirements to make content suitable for children will make online services less useful. Not being able freely to express and receive ideas and information is itself a harm. It is a huge price to pay for authorities being unable to take responsibility for law enforcement, reconcile to losing political battles or trust people to be able to make decisions for themselves and their families.

5   LIBERTY: BEYOND LEFT OR RIGHT?

Claire Fox

Free speech is in crisis, with far too few allies. Who to blame? The obvious answer is the left. After all, for over a decade, the left has driven some of the most egregiously illiberal assaults on free expression. One of the most galling aspects of contemporary politics is the casual way that freedom has been dubbed as right wing – as though left-wing ideas are antithetical to liberty. Whenever I argue that free speech should be a priority, left-leaning peers sneeringly label me as a libertarian; in their minds this label cancels out any previous left-wing credentials. However, the modern left's decision to treat liberty as a dodgy term of opprobrium is a betrayal of its own roots in Enlightenment thought. Worse, it flatters the right, which likes to see itself as the true champion of freedom but has too many skeletons in its own cupboard to claim this convincingly.

In truth, distrust in the *demos* has united both left and right, albeit in different time frames, driven by different motivations and rhetoric. From the eighteenth and nineteenth centuries, the right deployed both elitist authoritarianism and moralistic paternalism to contain self-determining urges associated with the emergence of mass society. Latterly, in the twentieth century, the left became disillusioned with the masses' susceptibility to 'false consciousness'. To counter a working class that it considered too easily duped by right-wing or populist ideas, the left worldwide embraced censorship to limit access to the wrong ideas. For both left and right, the instinct to ban and silence has been fuelled by a suspicion that the public needs help to arrive at 'correct' views, by limiting the choice of ideas to which they have access.

Seeing liberty and free speech through left/right lenses has limitations. It is too easy to get stuck in political categories which have run out of steam and relevance. But to understand why free speech is so fragile today, and to fight off contemporary 'cancel culture', we need to acknowledge that both left and right have, over different periods in history, embraced censorious ideas. Neither has consistently cultivated a deep commitment to liberty as the cornerstone of democracy. This explains why today, across the political spectrum, free speech is considered second order, a negotiable and dispensable nicety, easily sidelined when society faces huge challenges, no more so than in times of crisis. Two recent scenarios illustrate the point.

Free speech and the Covid-19 crisis

In an emergency such as a pandemic, when society faces a genuinely frightening and unpredictable threat, freedom of speech should be an invaluable asset. In the face of Covid-19, even the most ardent freedom lovers – whether left or right – have been prepared to allow governments worldwide to impose temporary restrictions on everyday freedoms, motivated by a sense of social solidarity. However, it has been telling to see the ease with which so many have celebrated the imposition of some of the most draconian powers we have seen in the modern era. When lockdown was enacted, the *Guardian*'s Owen Jones bizarrely tweeted 'Never thought I'd be relieved to be placed under house arrest along with millions of people under a police state by a right wing Tory government'.[1]

Owen's relief at house arrest may have been extreme, but he was not alone on the left in endorsing lockdown. Labour and trade union activists denounced libertarianism, insisting that even a Conservative-led state's lockdown was a safer bet than trusting the majority of free individuals to do the right thing voluntarily.

While many were reluctantly lending their support to such illiberal restrictions, it became all the more urgent and necessary to be vigilant about the use of these extraordinary measures, and to allow maximum space for debate and discussion. Free thinking and free speech should be invaluable tools in affording the public the capacity to question (not necessarily to oppose) the efficacy of government responses, which entailed the dramatic re-organisation of social and economic life. We needed to be free at least to query whether particular suspensions of our liberties or the oppressive policing of those breaching rules, were always appropriate or proportionate.

---

1   https://twitter.com/OwenJones84/status/1242219020625076226?s=20

When facing a new virus, and told we must listen to experts, free speech is a democratic asset. Even when locked in at home, the public could at least use new technology to hear a variety of voices from medicine and science, to assess the often contradictory evidence from virologists and behavioural scientists around the globe. While we may have been told to socially distance, we could form a sense of community dialogue via Zoom, Facebook and Twitter and not be cut off from the full range of opinions. The temporary physical lockdown may have been endurable if our freedom to speak and debate was not locked down as well. What happened, however, morphed into a free speech battle.

The Covid narrative is controlled by the new elites

Initially, the Conservative government suggested it would treat the British public as grownups and trust us to comply with the new rules. But as lockdown afforded millions of us the time to investigate this new virus, debates started to open up as people realised that the notion of 'the' science – with one immutable truth – was a myth. It became apparent to all that theories, whether of herd immunity or the effectiveness of mask-wearing, were not settled questions. The public started to have intelligent exchanges outside officialdom's control.

Politicians began to realise that the public might alight on theories at odds with the official UK line on the virus. They could at this stage have concluded that even if our physical health was in peril, at least a healthy democratic spirit of inquiry remained at liberty. Instead, the response was to shut discussions down, on the assumption that a gullible public could not be trusted to make up its own mind by having access to each and every hypothesis.

One mechanism for reining in discussion was to recruit Big Tech companies as Thought Police, appointing them the arbiters of what could and could not be said on their various platforms about the nature of the virus and the best ways to fight the threat it posed. Many assumed that the main concern of the owners of new media platforms would be to shut down cranky conspiracy-mongers, anti-vaxxers and 5G obsessives (all of whom, by the way, should be able to flaunt their wacky wares in the public square). Instead, policing Covid debate took a more sinister turn, deciding which scientists were valid, and cancelling the voices of respected experts just because they wouldn't comply with the outlooks of different national political elites. In one infamous early instance of overt censorship, more than 5 million watched and discussed an hour-long video featuring Dan Erickson and Artin Massihi, two doctors who run a private urgent-care clinic in Bakersfield, California, suggesting Covid-19 death tolls were being boosted and that lockdowns might do more harm than good. Fair comment, surely, from two respectable medics? Yet YouTube removed the video because they claimed that it violated their user policy, by disputing the official health narrative.[2]

---

2   https://www.turnto23.com/news/coronavirus/video-interview-with-dr
    -dan-erickson-and-dr-artin-massihi-taken-down-from-youtube

For Facebook, any scientific opinions disputing the official recommendations of the World Health Organization were dubbed misinformation (despite WHO's own evidence being considered contentious and contradictory within scientific and political circles internationally). The social media company's 'VP of Integrity', Guy Rosen, provided *An Update on Our Work to Keep People Informed and Limit Misinformation About COVID-19.*[3] It makes chilling reading:

> We're going to start showing messages in News Feed to people who have liked, reacted or commented on harmful misinformation about COVID-19 that we have since removed. These messages will connect people to COVID-19 myths debunked by the WHO including ones we've removed from our platform for leading to imminent physical harm. We want to connect people who may have interacted with harmful misinformation about the virus with the truth from authoritative sources in case they see or hear these claims again off of [sic] Facebook.

Even government-approved scientists have complained about censoring what the public get told. Before being released to the public in May 2020, a report that summarised SAGE (Scientific Advisory Group on Emergencies) discussions about how to handle social distancing measures had almost a page and a half of text so heavily redacted that it was virtually unreadable. Ironically, the report was

---

3   https://about.fb.com/news/2020/04/covid-19-misinfo-update/

published in an attempt to mollify criticism about the lack of transparency over advice given to ministers. In response Stephen Reicher (2020), Professor of Social Psychology at the University of St Andrews said

> The greatest asset we have in this crisis is the trust and adherence of the public. You want trust? You need to be open with people. This isn't open. It is reminiscent of Stalinist Russia. Not a good look.

However, members of SAGE were in a weak position to complain, because they themselves, along with Silicon Valley authorities, acted as a modern-day Star Chamber. This new clerisy has proved all too willing to create a climate conducive to shaming members of the public who won't comply with official 'advice'. The non-redacted minutes of the SAGE behavioural science group (SPI-B) for 23 March 2020 suggested '[c]onsider use of social disapproval for failure to comply'. And that strategy of cultivating 'social disapproval' – that is stirring up citizens and state agencies to shame and ultimately silence non-compliance – has been all too successful.

Demonising dissidents

These days, explicit state censorship is a rarity, but informal silencing of people often takes insidious forms.[4] Perfectly reasonable views are caricatured as extremist and

---

4   As I explain in Fox (2018).

delegitimised as beyond the pale while individuals who don't toe any number of orthodox lines are mislabelled and demonised. The elite's handling of public discussion on Covid followed this pattern: it encouraged social disapproval and created a mood of intolerance aimed at anyone who failed to endorse public health messaging.

A mood of intolerance was backed up by real powers given to councils and police forces, who in turn often deployed a mean-spirited approach to any deviation from following the minutiae of rules (not laws). Some police forces set up hotlines so that people could report their neighbours for breaking lockdown. A spate of menacing Twitter posts by various police forces made everything from sunbathing in the park to excessive walking in the countryside subject to threats of on-the-spot fines or worse.

It wasn't just minor rule-breaking that led to a disproportionate response. People who spoke out against regulations, often introduced with little or no parliamentary scrutiny, were damned as selfish psychopaths who didn't care if the elderly died. Even mildly sceptical questions were declared out of order and within a mere few weeks of the pandemic being declared, those who dared challenge any aspect of an increasingly rigid and strictly enforced lockdown-orthodoxy were being vilified. Lockdown sceptics such as Toby Young, Allison Pearson and Peter Hitchens were routinely pilloried and hounded, labelled as crackpots and 'Covid deniers'. Whether one found their views wacky, sinister or downright daft matters less than the illiberal attempts at delegitimising their opinions as too dangerous to be listened to by the public.

Ordinary people – at this stage understandably gripped by fear of a deadly virus – were expected passively to consume daily press conferences in which Conservative ministers, like benevolent parents, would tell them how to behave and what to think. No doubt the majority accepted this, at least initially; many fearful, others keen to do whatever it would take to defeat the virus. But assessing the public mood is hard to read when dissent is pathologised as representing 'sociopathic symptoms and antisocial traits'.[5] Rendering certain views as beyond the pale of mainstream discourse will be familiar to anyone who voted Leave in the EU referendum; this 'us versus them' narrative lumps anyone who does not repeat government mantras to the letter as akin to the maddest elements on the fringes of society. Such toxic tactics ensure that the public becomes wary of being branded as mad or bad for saying the wrong thing.

Speech as violence

Political responses to Covid reoriented society around the principle of safety, ensuring every other political and social freedom was downgraded. Prioritising safety over freedom has a long history: national security and anti-terrorism

---

5   In August last year British newspapers reported one Brazilian research study that suggested these dissidents were exhibiting sociopathic symptoms and antisocial traits, such as low levels of empathy and high levels of callousness, deceitfulness and risk-taking. See, for example, Refusal to wear a facemask linked to sociopathy. *The Times*, 31 August 2020 (https://www.thetimes.co.uk/article/refusal-to-wear-a-facemask-linked-to-socio pathy-69zr7hcqh).

legislation are routinely used to compromise free speech. But even then, physical violence and harm has generally been treated as a different order issue to speech, however aggressive. No matter how incendiary words might be, historically it was accepted that they were not bullets or knives.

But over the last decade harm and safety were seen as more nebulous concepts; words have increasingly been taken as equivalent to physical violence and are policed accordingly. In recent years, the intensifying campus free speech wars have revealed how J. S. Mill's harm principle has become an ever-expansive category to justify censorship, usually deploying the language of mental health to justify silencing offensive views considered harmful psychologically. Some groups of students have demanded that college authorities provide safe spaces to protect vulnerable minorities from the psychological damage inflicted by 'assaultive speech'. Speakers are no-platformed and disinvited because it is alleged their views will lead to trauma – as opposed to merely challenging or discomfiting the student. Universities use trigger warnings for fear that certain topics might trigger post-traumatic stress disorder or symptoms of emotional distress.[6] Free speech has been so pathologised it has been given a medical diagnosis. In an article aptly entitled 'When is speech violence?', Lisa Feldman Barrett (2017), a professor of psychology, wrote, 'Words can have a powerful effect on your nervous system. Certain types of adversity, even

6   Ibid.

those involving no physical contact, can make you sick ... shorten your life.'

The slippery-slope elision of speech and violence reached a new phase with the coming of the Covid pandemic. The official responses to Covid and the focus on safety and protection consolidated the trend of viewing ideas as dangerous. In the minutes of the SAGE behavioural science group (SPI-B) for 23 March, one recommendation was to '[u]se media to increase sense of personal threat'. Now speech is presented as a literal, visceral threat to physical well-being; dissenting opinions castigated as potentially being responsible for deaths. This strategy successfully created a culture of fear and led to the accusation that 'dangerous misinformation spreaders' are 'tantamount to accessories to manslaughter'. In this context, anyone who expresses the wrong views can be perceived as a threat to life. *ByLine Times* editor Peter Jukes took it upon himself to declare which views were safe to tweet and which were dangerous, concluding 'I hope this wave of Covid-Denialism retreats fast, but how many lives have been put in danger in their wake?'[7]

Covid conclusions

Silkie Carlo, director of the campaign group Big Brother Watch, has warned that Covid lockdown legislation amounts to 'the greatest loss of liberty in modern Britain

---

7   https://twitter.com/peterjukes/status/1300849367977545735?s=20,
    https://twitter.com/peterjukes/status/1300549363161329671?s=20,
    https://twitter.com/peterjukes/status/1303440798575398916?s=20

and it has happened by diktat. This is how autocracies and dictatorships emerge, for the "greater good", measure by measure.'[8] At the very least, such extraordinary changes deserve the widest possible political debate. Yet a Conservative prime minister, a self-described libertarian, has allowed a mood of intolerance to act as his policies' enforcer. Free speech was casually discarded in an effort to ensure that government public health messages were uncritically followed by compliant citizens. Alternative views, nuance, questions were decried as irresponsible, anti-science, fake news, even lethal. As open-minded free speech became one of the main casualties of the Tories' handling of the pandemic, right-wingers' boast that they are the keepers of the liberty flame look laughable. To compound the problem, another crisis came along, and yet again the default position became an assault on free speech, this time led by the left.

The racism crisis and the threats to free thought and expression

During the lockdown, the brutal death of George Floyd in the US sparked another type of crisis. A genuine, furious, international reaction to events in Minneapolis initially seemed a historic moment that could launch a deeper discussion about how to achieve social change, uniting people in fighting discrimination and injustice.

---

8   Quoted in Liberty in lockdown. *The Critic*, September 2020 (https://thecritic.co.uk/liberty-in-lockdown/).

Could this be a chance to reaffirm a commitment to Martin Luther King's dream of treating people according to the content of their character and not the colour of their skin? Sadly not; indeed such a colour-blind approach has itself been denounced as racist and the subject of the 'you can't say that' culture. The left, caught in the vice-like grip of postmodernism, critical race theory and identity politics, has shown that its first instinct is to close down, not open up, debate. Rather than initiating a broader discussion about racism, the George Floyd moment quickly turned into a quagmire of censorious intolerance, with undertones of McCarthyism. This reaction created an atmosphere in which not only 'racist' statues were being toppled; a range of cultural artefacts, TV series, celebrities, columnists and controversial broadcasters were 'cancelled' too.

Things spiralled out of control so quickly, that left-leaning liberals and veteran civil libertarians began to speak out against the growing intolerance on the left. In July, 153 prominent writers, academics and celebrities, spanning across ideologies, signed a letter in *Harper's Magazine*.[9] People such as Noam Chomsky, Gloria Steinem, J. K. Rowling and Salman Rushdie expressed concern that 'the free exchange of information and ideas, the lifeblood of a liberal society, is daily becoming more constricted'. The response? Many of the signatories' left-wing peers, along with Black Lives Matters activists, attacked the alleged straw-man nature of the letter's complaints and denied that cancel culture existed. Eventually, with dull predictability, these

---

9   https://harpers.org/a-letter-on-justice-and-open-debate/

critics proceeded to vilify, caricature and ironically try to cancel the letter's signatories for their temerity in opposing censorious trends.

The fast and furious way that an opportunity to have an open and constructive discussion about racism turned into a censorship-fest, far removed from the sad death of Mr Floyd, illustrated just how fragile free speech has become – immediately dispensed with in the name of the greater good. This time, the cause was not state-endorsed safetyism as with Covid, but how to enshrine a particular narrative on racism.

Demonising dissidents again

As with Covid, the method for enforcing conformity around a predetermined narrative has been by the demonisation of dissenting views. A McCarthyite threat to jobs has been added to the mix. The *Harper's* letter was a direct response to 'six weeks at American media and cultural institutions, which had experienced a wave of firings, resignations, and castigations over purportedly harmful words, deeds, and sometimes costumes'. While not so intense in the UK, similar threats have hung here above people's livelihoods and reputations, inhibiting free speech.

Almost overnight many left-wingers went from leading moral panics focused on too many travelling on the tube or a failure to enforce social distancing rules, to subjecting anyone who dared criticise the myriad BLM mass gatherings – even if they broke the same lockdown rules – to accusations of racism.

For example, Martin Shipton, chief reporter for the *Western Mail*, was asked to step down as a 'Wales Book of the Year' judge over tweets questioning why the demonstrations were being allowed to take place during lockdown. He said that these demos were exercises in 'virtue-signalling' and expressed concern about the effect they might have on the spread of Covid-19. That was enough for a well-regarded journalist to be publicly accused of white privilege and racist insensitivity. A Twitter pile-on, amounting to an ill-founded character assassination, was enough for Literature Wales to conclude that Martin Shipton's 'aggressive language' was 'detrimental' to the organisation's values. Shipton explained:

> After expressing my concerns about the Black Lives Matter protest in Cardiff, which undoubtedly broke the Welsh Government's prohibition on public gatherings of more than two people, I was subjected on Twitter to a vicious tirade of abuse and bullying that lasted for days ... Many of the tweets questioned my right to express an opinion, called into question my credentials as a journalist.[10]

This absurd and intolerant over-reaction by Literature Wales, in bowing to a Twitter mob rather than defending one of their own judges from abuse, was not an exception. Similarly, it took only 465 signatures on a Change.org petition for trustees of the award-winning charity Mancunian Way to

---

10 Black Lives Matter: Book judge axed over Twitter remarks. BBC News, 5 June 2020 (https://www.bbc.co.uk/news/uk-52940249).

sack its own CEO – indeed its founder – Nick Buckley MBE. His crime was to post a blog critiquing the Black Lives Matter manifesto. The boss of a charity, which aims to help children in Manchester avoid gang culture, faced the indignity of being labelled a bigot and having his motives maligned, as well as losing his job. Buckley was eventually reinstated after he fought back with the help of the Free Speech Union.[11] Notably, however, trade unions and left-wing activists, who historically prided themselves on championing workers' rights, were silent about this unfair sacking.[12]

While most people don't face being sacked for their views, the fear of the social repercussions of being (falsely) called-out as a racist at work if you, for example, haplessly ask if 'all lives matter' or challenge orthodoxies such as white fragility, has inevitably chilled free speech. Overall, the recent censorious tactic of demonisation has become both more entrenched and expanded since George Floyd's death, as the ideological contours of identity politics have become unquestionable. Anyone who dares criticise Black Lives Matter is treated as a heretic. The heretic-hunters present themselves as grassroots campaigners, attacking privilege. However, they are increasingly in positions of power and can impose their narrative on the rest of society.

---

11 Fired charity boss restored. *The Critic*, 23 July 2020 (https://thecritic.co.uk/fired-charity-boss-restored/).

12 Indeed, astonishingly, it is often self-described left-wingers who now justify, and even lead the calls for, bosses to discipline employees for expressing views they deem unacceptable. As Tom Slater (2020) notes: 'In the culture wars of today, the illiberal left's primary response to any statement it disagrees with seems to be demanding that the person who said it be immediately sacked and made an example of.'

The identity narrative is controlled by the new elite

'Cancelling' people is often posited as a valid 'punching up' strategy that turns the tables on the powerful.[13] However, in some ways, what we have seen since Floyd's death is a consolidation of a power grab by an elite. If with Covid the new technocratic clerisy charged with policing speech were Internet companies or officially sanctioned scientists, the BLM enforcers are the managerial class which runs cultural, media, educational and corporate organisations. It was not disadvantaged people on the street who determined change, but rather middle-class people in comfortable public sector or quasi-public sector jobs who took the knee and took the initiative.

The new prescriptive narrative that emerged during the BLM summer of 2020 was dictated by Critical Race Theory (CRT) (see, for instance, Chakrabaty et al. 2014). Once largely confined to leftist academic circles, CRT went mainstream. This obscurantist theory determines that institutions are inherently racist and that race itself is a 'socially constructed concept that is used by white people to further their economic and political interests at the expense of people of colour'.[14] White people have unearned 'white privilege' granted merely by their skin colour, whether they know it or not, and even if they are

13 See, for example, comments made by Nesrine Malik and Zoe Williams in *The Guardian*, 8 July 2020 (https://www.theguardian.com/commentis free/2020/jul/08/is-free-speech-under-threat-cancel-culture-writers-res pond).

14 https://www.britannica.com/topic/critical-race-theory

homeless and poor. Previously anti-racist values, such as equal treatment or meritocracy, are written off as tools for maintaining white power.

Often those who are targets of educative interventions from top-down management are millions of ordinary people unfamiliar with the CRT identity tropes so beloved of today's new left. This exercise, reminiscent of the Chinese Cultural Revolution, involves 're-educating' the public on what constitutes bigotry and adjusting everything in the public realm to reflect new sensibilities. It is being conducted with no debate or democratic mandate. Censorious schemes to remodel citizens and employees so that they follow an approved anti-racist script, derive their radical dynamism from claims that this is the rebalancing power in favour of oppressed voices. Ironically, this means 'othering' the majority as ignorant.

In some ways activists are right: before George Floyd, the public were ignorant of the mores and linguistic niceties of identitarianism that have consumed universities over the last decade. As the culture wars burst open the lockdown, spilled onto the streets and took over the popular domain, the British public has watched aghast. Often feelings of shock, alienation and fury – expressed for example in demonstrations against statues being pulled down, or using the retort that surely 'ALL lives matter' – were used as proof that the vast majority – often working class people – needed a lesson in correct thinking.

For example, unless you followed the #RhodesMustFall movement that preoccupied Oxford University a few years ago – and morphed into a wider 'decolonise the curriculum' campaign across higher education – you might have been bewildered by the rush to depose inanimate objects as though they are actively playing a role in the treatment of black people today. Those who objected were labelled as a part of what Owen Jones described in a *Guardian* column as 'a weaponised backlash from the right'.[15] Jones rejoiced in the idea that 'the country has been dragged into a mass history lesson, and the lecturers standing at the front of class are young black protesters and their allies'.

Those radicals who know better used the crisis to re-educate those with the 'wrong' perspectives on race by implementing far-reaching changes aimed at cancelling swathes of knowledge and replacing them with an approved version of reality. The way that almost every major institution or organisation is reorganising itself around this new narrative is well documented. Museums and art galleries are now rewriting all the descriptors of their artefacts, and removing items said to cause offence. Visitors can't be trusted to simply look at objects or artworks. They must interpret them in a particular way, as dictated by the new experts – not so much curators based in deep disciplinary knowledge, but curators of attitudinal correctness, as dictated by the tenets of diversity and CRT. For example, the mission of the British Library – once straightforwardly a repository of universal knowledge for all – is now declared by its chief librarian as needing a 'major cultural

15 Toppling statues of bygone tyrants forces British people to face present-day racism. *The Guardian*, 11 June 2020 (https://www.theguardian.com/com mentisfree/2020/jun/11/toppling-statues-bygone-tyrants-forces-british -people-face-present-day-racism).

change' as dictated by reforms proposed by a 'Decolonising Working Group'.[16]

What was most striking about events at the British Library was the shift to a root-and-branch re-education programme aimed at correcting the false consciousness espoused by its own employees. White staff were asked to educate themselves about their apparent privilege, so they could understand, for example, that a belief in 'one human family' was 'covert white supremacy'. They were given a prescriptive reading list to that end, presumably excluding all those books dating back centuries which they are charged with preserving for the nation.

Posing as anti-establishment rebels, the left are relishing this cultural coup. Indeed, they are increasingly influencing those in power, or themselves assuming positions of power. Changes in the Civil Service illustrate the point. In an unlikely site for revolution, mandarins at the heart of Whitehall came out as enthusiasts of Critical Race Theory, launching a full-scale struggle session to root out 'systemic racism', 'white privilege' and 'white fragility' from its own ranks. According to an article in *The Critic*,[17] the

---

16 These included the 'urgent and overdue need to reckon fully and openly with the colonial origins and legacy of some of the library's historic collections and practices'; even the BL building itself was denounced as an 'imperialism symbol' because it is said to resemble a battleship. British Library's chief librarian says 'racism is the creation of white people' as bosses call for changes to displays in wake of BLM movement after colleagues were 'urged to support the work of Labour MP Diane Abbott'. *Daily Mail*, 30 August 2020 (https://www.dailymail.co.uk/news/article-8678577/British-Librarys-chief-librarian-says-racism-creation-white-people.html).

17 The BLM takeover of Whitehall. *The Critic*, 18 August 2020 (https://thecritic.co.uk/blm-is-a-politically-contentious-issue/).

Lockdown BLM upheaval saw the Permanent Secretary of the Department for Education, Jonathan Slater, declaring his quest to 'tackle the whiteness of Senior Whitehall', tweeting the Black Lives Matter hashtag. This project even has personnel committed to raising race-consciousness. 'Project Race' and the 'Race Ambassadors Network' is a cohort of civil servants trained to operate on the 'ground level' and 'get those conversations happening, to hold people to account'. For holding people to account, read checking on what people say, and presumably correcting those who misspeak. Or reporting them to the authorities. Or sending them on re-education courses.[18]

The favoured re-education method that emerged over this BLM summer was mandatory unconscious bias training, now being widely adopted across workplaces in the public and private sector. Unconscious bias is a theory that infers that anyone who has white skin cannot escape their unconscious bias, and needs to be trained, like Pavlov's dogs, to respond differently. Anyone who objects is invariably accused of failing to come to terms with their white privilege, proving that they are exactly the sort of people in need of re-education. This is the logic of witch-hunts through the ages.

If in the 1970s and 80s an earlier generation of 'progressives' patronisingly saw themselves as consciousness-raisers battling with the alleged false consciousness of workers who refused to be persuaded of the virtues of

---

18 The drive to purge the Civil Service of wrong-think predates the lockdown. For example, 39,826 civil servants have received unconscious bias training in the past five years.

socialism, now we have a new cadre of unconscious bias trainers. They assume that backward ideas are no longer rooted in the public realm of society and political ideology (where they can be debated) but lurk in the darkest recesses of individuals' psyches. Racism is reduced to a psychological, unconscious condition that people are not even aware of.

Instead of weighing up the merit of someone's publicly expressed opinions, judgement is now usurped by algorithmic Implicit Association Tests that, it is claimed, provide accurate measurement of unconscious racial bias. But despite deploying scientific jargon, the reliability of these tests is widely contested, with many reputable psychology studies showing that evidence of their success falls well below the normal threshold of experimental standards.[19]

Regardless of the unproven nature of this pseudo-science, unconscious bias training is now a multi-billion dollar industry worldwide. But what it signifies is an acknowledgement that many on the left have effectively given up on the project of using reason to persuade others. People cannot be trusted to know their own minds or to change their views by debate. The public is seen as a problem to be 'improved' by expert trainers. Argument, intellectual struggle and agency are replaced by standardised testing. The training people receive often amounts to little more than being instructed in following a preordained script.

---

19 For example, respected science writer Tom Chivers (2020) claims that companies spend a fortune on implicit bias tests – but they are next to useless.

'Silence is violence', mandated speech and bad faith

Following that script is now compulsory. While modern censorship has demanded that 'You Can't Say That', we are now faced with an additional new command: 'You Must Say THIS'. BLM's menacing slogan 'Silence is violence' demands that people are compelled to speak out on racism; staying quiet is itself characterised as dangerous. Breaking people's silence is not a call to develop arguments that might inspire people to speak out, but a demand that unless you sign up to vocal activism NOW, you will be damned as somehow complicit in racist brutality.[20] Just as loose talk on Covid was deemed harmful and therefore subject to regulation, silence is now deemed harmful. Quoted in an aptly titled article, Savala Trepczynski (2020), executive director of the Center for Social Justice at UC Berkeley, states: 'White silence is ... not neutral. It acts like a weapon. It's not even silent. It speaks volumes, right?'

The consequence of this is that discussion about serious issues such as racism has been reduced to little more than parroting a formulaic script or being put under pressure to demonstrate you are on the correct side via ubiquitous hashtags and symbols, such as putting a black square around Instagram messages. Those who don't conform face being shunned, cancelled or publicly shamed. A

---

20 A website statement for #ShutDownSTEM day (10 June 2020) declared 'unless you engage directly with eliminating racism, you are perpetuating it'. This statement is not designed to win hearts and minds to the cause of anti-racism. Instead, its purpose is to emphasise that from now on, political activity is not optional.

recently viral video of mobs shouting 'white silence is violence' descending on people eating out in Washington, demanding that diners raise a fist to support the movement, was chilling (see, for example, Turley 2020). Of course, many complied as protestors screamed in their faces. But even in its more mundane form, such as being compelled to have 'healthy conversations' about race, initiated by race ambassadors, as advocated in some universities,[21] it is a recipe for self-censorship. If forced to speak in bad faith, what happens to conscience or conscientious objection?

Beyond left and right: a new movement?

When their own speech is curated by others and stifled by a demand that dissenting views are dangerous, people unsurprisingly feel the need to conceal their opinions out of fear of a potential backlash. This affects people across the political divide.[22] There is, of course, no top-down, right-wing, authoritarian conspiracy or Marxist plot to censor ideas. However, the historically feeble commitment to free speech from left and right means that censorship, in its myriad forms, has too easily become the default position.

---

21 As detailed in Training students into a woke Stasi. *Spiked Online*, 14 January 2020 (https://www.spiked-online.com/2020/01/14/turning-students -into-a-woke-stasi/).

22 In a US survey in July 2020, the percentage of those who feared for their job prospects because of their views was similar across political lines: 34 per cent of conservatives, 31 per cent of liberals and 30 per cent of moderates 'worry they could miss out on job opportunities or get fired if their political views became known' (https://www.cato.org/publications/survey-reports/ poll-62-americans-say-they-have-political-views-theyre-afraid-share).

It is frequently leaned on by those in power, or by those with aspirations to seize power, to usurp the messy business of winning consent to implement change. Winning hearts and minds requires the effort of persuading people. Far easier to coerce agreement by making the desired narrative unquestionable.

The crisis in free speech is a far greater long-term threat to society than any virus. We need a new movement – beyond left or right – organised around freedom: committed to trusting the public with each and every opinion; to seeing our fellow citizens as equals and equal to the task of discerning their own views through guaranteeing access to unlimited, freely expressed ideas, however dangerous they may seem.

6   HAVING A LAUGH? FREE SPEECH IN COMEDY

Leo Kearse

When we think about freedom of speech in comedy, we might think of Lenny Bruce being led in shackles from the stage, a social media storm cancelling Kevin Hart from the Oscars, or Islamists gunning down satirical cartoonists. This is external censorship. Self-censorship is constant and invisible, though affected by external factors such as laws, audience response and the risk of being gunned down by Islamists.

In this chapter I look at the history of censorship in comedy, examine the different ways freedom of speech is affected and the consequences. I also tell of my own personal experience of being banned from my Fringe festival venue following allegations of transphobia, and of performing secret underground comedy shows in countries where autocratic regimes have banned them.

A brief history of censorship in comedy

Throughout history people have recognised the value of speaking truth to power through comedy. The powerful, meanwhile, have recognised the value of censoring jokers who undermine their authority. Socrates (who had been mocked in *The Clouds*, a comedy by Aristophanes) said at his trial that 'the laughter of the theatre was a harder task to answer than the arguments of my accusers'. Yet the powerful have also recognised the value comedy has in society – in defusing tensions, providing entertainment and letting people feel free.

Satire (the use of humour, irony, exaggeration or ridicule to expose and criticise people's stupidity or vices) is recorded in ancient Egypt: a satirical papyrus hanging in the British Museum dates from roughly 1100 BC (Berens 2014). In Greece the comic plays of Aristophanes date from around 420 BC (Roman and Roman 2010: 81). Aristophanes received censure – the Athenian general Cleon in particular was repeatedly mocked in his plays and in return criticised them, denouncing one play, *The Babylonians*, as slander.

The Roman satirist Juvenal introduced a more aggressive satire directed at specific iniquities 'in which the speaker attacks vice and error with contempt and indignation'[1] and was duly exiled.

In medieval Europe, early satire came from the clowns and jesters. A comedian[2] recounts the (possibly apocryphal) legend of the Bouffon:

Medieval towns cast out of the city walls their 'impure' citizens (disabled, homosexual, mentally ill, disfigured,

---

1 Roxanne Kent-Drury offers a definition of ancient satire (no date) (https://www.nku.edu/~rkdrury/422/satire_terms.html).

2 Personal communication.

etc.) to fend for themselves in the wilderness. Once a year the 'acceptable people' living in the town would invite the exiles back for the hock-tide feast. The outcasts were allowed this one day to deride the beautiful people – walking behind them, mocking their clothes, their movement, their position in society. Exiles weren't protected by law, however, and could be beaten or even killed on a whim.

Just as today, causing offence had consequences.

Professional jesters have been recorded in many premodern societies – from the royal courts of medieval Europe to Rome (Allen 1870) and even the Aztecs. Mocking the powerful in court could be a lucrative profession, but also a dangerous one. Archibald Armstrong, jester to King James VI, was awarded the monopoly on tobacco pipe sales and 1,000 acres in Ireland, but his criticism of Lord Buckingham led to a threat of hanging. With typical comedian's impertinence he responded: 'Dukes had often been hanged for insolence but never fools for talking.' After mocking the height of powerful nobleman and future Archbishop of Canterbury William Laud, Armstrong was banished from the King's court, finding a new profession as a moneylender (Chisholm 1911).

Modern censorship

Comedy has always questioned convention, and the powerful have always retaliated. At the birth of modern comedy, this came from the state. Lenny Bruce was targeted by US authorities for using language they deemed so obscene that it threatened the fabric of society. His many arrests included one for using the Yiddish swearword 'schmuck', a level of offence that seems laughably quaint today. Police would stand at the edge of the stage during his performances; he was arrested onstage in Chicago in 1962. Comedy club owners who dared to book him were also arrested. He was barred from entering the UK in the public interest in 1963,[3] presumably lest he contaminate British audiences by saying 'schmuck' again.

As the noose tightened around his career and finances, with fewer clubs willing to risk booking him, he was reported as saying, 'If I get busted in New York, the freest city in the world, that will be the end of my career.' This fear became reality when he was arrested for a final time in New York in 1964 after undercover police officers sat in the audience during his performance. Bruce and the club owner were found guilty of obscenity six months later. He died from a morphine overdose while released on bail. Lenny Bruce was officially pardoned in 2003,[4] but state censorship of comedy continues to this day.

Following a period of cultural liberalisation, governments in the West are now tightening restrictions on speech in the name of protecting marginalised members of society from 'hate'. But hate crime laws are often vaguely worded and overreach. The Scottish National Party's controversial Hate Crime Bill was amended to remove a section criminalising public performance, but could still

---

3   'Offensive' is the new 'obscene'. *Time*, 22 December 2014 (https://time
    .com/3642530/50-years-lenny-bruce/).

4   New York pardons late Lenny Bruce. BBC News, 23 December 2003 (http://
    news.bbc.co.uk/2/hi/americas/3345229.stm).

criminalise comedians if a 'reasonable person' perceives them to be 'abusive' or 'stir up hatred' on the grounds of characteristics such as sexuality or ethnicity. And for the first time in British legal history, private conversations in the home are criminalised, raising the spectre of prosecutions for jokes told around the dinner table.[5]

French comedian and political activist Dieudonné has amassed a list of convictions (including for defamation, tax evasion and anti-Semitism) and been banned from several French cities.[6] He has advocated terrorism (endorsing the massacre at *Charlie Hebdo* by Islamists), his shows have featured Holocaust deniers, he allies himself with the far right and he uses an inverted Nazi salute on stage. While this might not sound uproariously funny, his treatment differs from that of old-school racist comedians of the 1970s. Bernard Manning was never arrested. Jim Davidson wasn't banned from British cities. Instead, they were made unfashionable by the new wave of alternative comedians.

Making behaviour unfashionable may be more successful than banning it, because of the effect of psychological reactance, 'the motivation to regain a freedom after it has been lost or threatened [which] leads people to resist the social influence of others' (Steindl et al. 2015: 205). This phenomenon almost invariably leads to censored material

5   https://thecritic.co.uk/how-the-hate-crime-bill-defies-scottish-tradition/

6   An act of cruelty: an audience with Dieudonné M'bala M'bala, the man behind the 'quenelle' salute. *The Independent*, 26 January 2014 (https://www.independent.co.uk/news/people/dieudonn-mbala-mbala-an-act-of-cruelty-9089178.html).

being far more widely seen. Psychological reactance can also have a contradictory effect on a comedian's self-censorship. Comedian Darius Davies recounts being told not to mention Magners, the sponsors of a comedy festival he appeared at. 'I went on stage and made fun of Magners – they'd put the seed in my head.' He was, he says, promptly banned from the festival.

And comedy is too subjective for the boundaries of acceptable behaviour to be clearly demarcated. Canadian comedian Mike Ward was fined \$42,000 after a Quebec tribunal found that he had violated the human rights of a disabled child singer with the line 'I didn't know what illness he had, so I googled it and it turns out he's just ugly'. In the ruling, judge Scott Hughes wrote: 'Unacceptable remarks in private do not automatically become lawful when delivered by a comedian in the public sphere ... the fact of having a forum imposes certain responsibilities.'[7]

In 2016, Scottish YouTuber Mark Meechan, better known as Count Dankula, posted a video of him training his girlfriend's pug to give a Nazi salute (or the closest approximation of a Nazi salute that a pug can muster) when Meechan said 'gas the Jews'. An online furore followed. Meechan was arrested for committing a hate crime, convicted of being 'grossly offensive'[8] and fined £800.

---

7   Comedian Mike Ward ordered to pay \$35,000 in punitive damages to Jérémy Gabriel. *Montreal Gazette*, 21 July 2016 (https://montrealgazette.com/news/local-news/comedian-mike-ward-ordered-to-pay-35000-in-punitive-damages-to-jeremy-gabriel).

8   Man guilty of hate crime for filming pug's 'Nazi salutes'. BBC News, 20 March 2018 (https://www.bbc.com/news/uk-scotland-glasgow-west-43478925).

While it's undeniably offensive, it is meant as a joke. The video doesn't promote Nazism as a positive thing. If it did, the joke wouldn't work – the humour hinges on the dichotomy between the cuteness of the pug and the absolute evil of the Nazis. The joke reinforces the idea that Nazis are evil. A similar incongruity is behind the humour in Mel Brooks's classic film *The Producers*, which features Broadway musical sequences such as 'Springtime for Hitler', which was criticised as offensive upon its release but is now lauded as a classic.

Prominent comedians such as David Baddiel and Ricky Gervais decried the conviction. But Meechan's castigation didn't end with the court case and sentence. He told me of his harassment by online vigilantes who

> took it upon themselves to harass me and my family, post my private information online, as well as harass my employers into firing me. Anytime I got a new job, my employer would always be discovered and then the harassment would begin again and I would be fired all over again. I tried 8 times to just get a regular job, but every single time I was fired, so I used the only thing available to me which was YouTube.

The threat of mob harassment was more dissuasive to Meechan than state censure. The Internet has drastically reduced the amount of effort it takes to protest about something. Previously, protesters would have to organise a group of people, transport them to a location, create placards, write letters, buy stamps. Now, an online petition can be autofilled with your contact info and sent with two clicks; employers can be harassed anonymously from a laptop.

Other censorship comes from pressure groups who try to influence government and broadcasters. Mary Whitehouse was the founder and first president of the National Viewers' and Listeners' Association, which campaigned against the publication and broadcast of offensive material. Mainstream comedians such as Benny Hill and Dave Allen were chastised for their profane language and sexualised content. Although Mrs Whitehouse was mocked for her outmoded puritanism, her campaigns led to stronger laws against obscenity on television, and the establishment of a watchdog group to raise standards in broadcasting.[9]

Some pressure groups take a more direct approach to material that offends them. The satirical anti-religious French magazine *Charlie Hebdo* drew the ire of Islamic groups when it published cartoons of the Prophet Muhammad alongside its caricatures of figureheads from other religions. Islamic organisations sued, unsuccessfully, under France's hate speech laws. This didn't dissuade the magazine, which featured a cartoon of the Prophet Muhammad on its cover in 2011. Later that year, its offices were destroyed by a bomb. *Charlie Hebdo*'s editor said the blasphemy would continue 'until Islam is just as banal as Catholicism'.[10] In 2015 armed Islamists stormed the new

---

9   Mary Whitehouse, 91; led British TV cleanup. *Los Angeles Times*, 26 November 2001 (https://www.latimes.com/archives/la-xpm-2001-nov-26-me-83 56-story.html).

10   The *Charlie Hebdo* affair: laughing at blasphemy. *New Yorker*, 28 September 2012 (https://www.newyorker.com/news/news-desk/the-charlie-hebdo-af fair-laughing-at-blasphemy).

offices, shooting twelve people (more were killed when the gunmen went on the run).

Public reaction was mixed; alongside the denunciations of violence and the worldwide slogan of support, 'Je suis Charlie', were accusations that the magazine's staff had brought this on themselves. France's Foreign Minister asked, 'Is it really sensible or intelligent to pour oil on the fire?'[11] *Charlie Hebdo* continued, however, with the first issue released after the attacks selling an estimated 3.5 million copies, a substantial increase on the usual weekly distribution of 60,000.

Comedians can also be censored by individuals who have been slandered. Comedian Louise Reay was sued for defamation by her estranged husband after she claimed in her comedy show that their relationship was abusive, identifying him in pictures and video. Louise became a minor cause célèbre and raised over £10,000 in donations to help fund her defence, eventually settling out of court.[12]

Industry censorship

Venues, clubs and live bookers can restrict comedians' freedom of speech by not booking them. Unless the decision is publicly announced, this can be hard to prove. A

---

11 French weekly defied advice to tone down despite threats. *Boston Globe*, 7 January 2015 (https://www.bostonglobe.com/news/world/2015/01/07/ charlie-hebdo-broke-taboos-defying-threats-and-violence/GtEKEuh IWEYuQivxHZAMUM/story.html).

12 Her gofundme site is https://www.gofundme.com/f/comedian-being-sued -free-speech.

handful of comedy nights, such as London's Quantum Leopard, proudly proclaim they do not give a platform to offensive acts, but they tend to be smaller nights for hobbyists rather than professionals (Quantum Leopard pays £5 per spot). In my experience, most professional bookers will put personal ideologies to one side and book acts who make audiences laugh and book tickets for the next show. They are, however, fearful of attention that could lead to negative publicity, venues being snubbed by audiences, or funding being cancelled.

Governments can censor comedy by direct involvement in the comedy industry. The ruling Scottish party, the Scottish National Party, controls the two main comedy clubs in Scotland (the Glasgow Stand and Edinburgh Stand are owned by SNP Member of Parliament Tommy Sheppard[13]). This dissuades Scottish comedians from criticising the SNP lest they damage their career.

Just like clubs, hosts for online comedy content – YouTube, Facebook, Twitter – can issue outright bans, as they have for alt-right comic Owen Benjamin, who has been banned from most social media platforms for anti-Semitism, white nationalism, transphobia and racism.[14]

Bans are rare, however. What are more usual, and less easy to spot, are shadow bans, where material that's considered offensive (but doesn't breach any guidelines) is simply hidden. Konstantin Kisin explains how this happened to

---

13 https://www.tommysheppardmp.scot/about/#team

14 Owen Benjamin, alt-right comedian, banned from YouTube. *Daily Dot*, 26 January 2021 (https://www.dailydot.com/layer8/owen-benjamin-you tube/).

an interview with Peter Hitchens on his podcast Trigger-nometry: 'Instead of deleting it and allowing us the right of appeal, they simply "hid" the interview from searches on YouTube and Google. Technically, the interview is still there – you just can't find it.'[15]

Social media platforms argue that they are commercially provided services; cutting access to them isn't censorship as people are free to use another service. But these platforms operate monopolistically: Facebook also owns Instagram and WhatsApp. Banning comedians from social media is denying them access to the ecosystem for public discourse. And social media platforms also argue, in a different context, that they have (and can have) no control over their content; this is part of the definition of 'platform' which gets them various legal advantages over publishers.[16] They want both to censor and to claim the advantages that come with being uncensoring.

Free speech can be affected by conditions imposed by organisers. I perform at all kinds of shows – from golf club after-dinner speeches, to cruise ships, to music festivals – because I love money. Many shows come with conditions: don't swear, no sexual references, don't mention the Sultan. But some conditions are more stultifying. After being invited to perform at an event at the School of Oriental and African Studies, Konstantin Kisin was

---

15 We must fight YouTube's outrageous censoring of lockdown sceptics. *The Telegraph*, 1 June 2021 (https://www.telegraph.co.uk/news/2020/06/01/mu st-fight-youtubes-outrageous-censoring-lockdown-sceptics/).

16 Free speech and the regulation of social media content. Congressional Research Services, 27 March 2019 (https://fas.org/sgp/crs/misc/R45650.pdf).

asked to sign a 'Behaviour Agreement Form' agreeing to the School's 'zero tolerance policy with regards to racism, sexism, classism, ageism, ableism, homophobia, biphobia, transphobia, xenophobia, Islamophobia or anti-religion or anti-atheism'.

Konstantin felt that he had no option but to cancel:

> I didn't turn down this gig because I'm some racist, homophobic, xenophobic, ableist comedian. I turned down this gig because if you sign a contract like that, you're exposing yourself to someone's bad interpretation. If someone writes a contract like that, the chances are that they will be hypersensitive, vigilant and trying to catch you out.[17]

Kisin's 'Behaviour Agreement Form' is emblematic of the politically correct 'woke' culture creeping out from liberal arts colleges to close its deadening, stultifying hands around the throat of contemporary discourse, according to established comedians such as Jerry Seinfeld, John Cleese, Mel Brooks and Chris Rock. Rock stopped playing colleges because 'they're way too conservative in their social views and their willingness not to offend anybody'.[18]

Jerry Seinfeld also says colleges are too politically correct, calling it 'anti-comedy'. He described political correctness as young people's posturing, saying, 'They just want to use these words. "That's racist. That's sexist. That's

---

17 Comedian refused to sign 'behavioural agreement' before gig. BBC News, 12 December 2018 (https://www.bbc.co.uk/news/newsbeat-46541002).

18 In conversation Chris Rock. *New York Vulture*, no date (https://www.vulture.com/2014/11/chris-rock-frank-rich-in-conversation.html).

prejudice." They don't even know what they're talking about.'[19]

Ironically, the liberal left in the past were often trying to stop censorship, campaigning to have controversial and seditious works of art shown in theatres, galleries and on television, and mocking the censors for being puritanical relics. Now, woke liberals are the puritans, condemning anything that fails to meet their exacting (yet frequently changing) dogma.

Comedians who complain that free speech is restricted by political correctness are often accused of nefarious intent. 'When comedians say: "Oh you can't say ANYTHING these days!", what they are actually saying is, "I don't know how to be funny without stomping on people,"' says non-binary woke comedian Sofie Hagen.[20] *Vice* magazine linked freedom of speech to fascism in an article about Comedy Unleashed, a free speech comedy night: 'By indulging the fiction that free speech for conservatives is threatened, the mainstream has allowed the far-right to carve out a new space in the culture.'[21]

---

19 Jerry Seinfeld says political correctness is killing comedy. *Jezebel*, 7 June 2015 (https://jezebel.com/jerry-seinfeld-says-political-correctness-is-kill ing-co-1709719818).

20 Is standup comedy doomed? The future of funny post-Kevin Hart, Louis CK and Nanette. *The Guardian*, 19 January 2019 (https://www.theguar dian.com/culture/2019/jan/19/is-standup-comedy-doomed-future-of -funny-kevin-hart-louis-ck-nanette).

21 Inside London's 'free speech' comedy night. *Vice*, 5 June 2019 (https:// www.vice.com/en_uk/article/xwn5w4/comedy-unleashed-london-free -speech-right-wing).

Censoring the recent past

Comedy that at the time of its creation is considered progressive can fall foul of the narrowing acceptabilities of future generations. The Black Lives Matter movement is an example of this; as it sent paroxysms through a society desperate to show its support, TV executives fell over themselves in a rush to remove or revise any comedy shows that might be considered racist.[22] *Fawlty Towers, Little Britain, The League of Gentlemen, Mighty Boosh, Come Fly With Me, The Simpsons, Bo Selecta* – all were considered unacceptable, usually because of depictions of blackface or racist language (even when, as in the case of *Fawlty Towers*, the language is used to indicate the outmoded views of a character). The removal of much-loved TV shows was seen by some as a 'culture war' with white British culture under attack.[23] Ironically, this might suggest the need for more BAME people in positions of power in the media, as a BAME executive would be less likely to remove a TV show out of a fear of looking insufficiently anti-racist.

Comedians are even trying to censor each other. In 2017 the American comedian Hari Kondabolu accused *The Simpsons* of racism, saying he was bullied at school

22 For shows that contain only a modicum of offensive material, a trigger warning at the outset is deemed a sufficient safeguard. For example, viewers of certain episodes of *The Good Life* are now warned that they may glimpse a Robinson's golly on an apron.

23 BBC removes iconic 'Don't Mention the War' episode from UKTV. *Express*, 12 June 2020 (https://www.express.co.uk/showbiz/tv-radio/1294758/faw lty-towers-bbc-remove-dont-mention-the-war-episode-uktv-black-lives -matter-racism).

because of the character Apu, who was voiced by white actor Hank Azaria. And the character Apu undeniably does rely on easy stereotypes – as does every single other character in *The Simpsons*. Groundskeeper Willie is potentially hugely offensive to Scottish people. Apu was subsequently dropped from the series, though later reinstated without Azaria's voice.

Offstage actions

Comedians are being censored for what they do offstage as well as what they say onstage. Allegations of sexual assault against the comedian Bill Cosby dating back decades rose to prominence in 2014 after being highlighted in a viral standup routine by the comedian Hannibal Buress.[24] Fittingly, Buress was responding to Cosby's public moralising about young black men like himself. Cosby's live performances were beleaguered by heckles, protests and public opprobrium until he finally quit performing just a few months before his conviction in 2018.

American comedian Louis CK was accused of, and admitted to, sexually harassing female colleagues by masturbating in front of them and over the phone. Although never formally charged, public outcry forced him to take an extended hiatus from live performances and the release of his Hollywood film, *I Love You Daddy*, was cancelled. When

---

24 Hannibal Buress: how a comedian reignited the Bill Cosby allegations. *The Guardian*, 26 April 2018 (https://www.theguardian.com/world/2018/apr/26/hannibal-buress-how-a-comedian-reignited-the-bill-cosby-allegations).

he made a tentative return to live performance, protests forced the cancellation of shows. The Leeds-based promoter Toby Jones said, 'The sheer amount of hatred from both the industry and members of the public made running the shows utterly untenable.'[25]

Comedians have also been called out for hypocrisy in their actions. Aziz Ansari fell from grace in 2018 when a woman published a blog accusing him of sexual misconduct on a date (she recounts Ansari pushing for sex despite her indicating her lack of interest).[26] Some see his misdeeds as less serious than CK's,[27] but Ansari isn't in Motley Crue. He's a man who's gone to great lengths to stress his woke feminist credentials, even writing a feminist dating book, *Modern Romance*, accompanied by promotional interviews where he professed, 'I've been a feminist my whole life.'[28] For him to then pressure an unresponsive woman for sex and treat her (in her words) as if he's a 'horny, entitled 18 year old' understandably rankles with people.

However, Ansari's career recovered from his sexual misconduct allegations, and was perhaps even boosted by

---

25 Louis CK's UK gigs dropped after protests. *Chortle* (no date) (https://www.chortle.co.uk/news/2019/05/15/43048/louis_cks_uk_gigs_dropped_after_backlash).

26 I went on a date with Aziz Ansari. It turned into the worst night of my life. *Babe* (no date) (https://babe.net/2018/01/13/aziz-ansari-28355).

27 Aziz Ansari is guilty. Of not being a mind reader. *New York Times*, 15 January 2015 (https://www.nytimes.com/2018/01/15/opinion/aziz-ansari-babe-sexual-harassment.html).

28 Aziz Ansari: 'I've always been a feminist. There wasn't a period when I was against women and then started dating one.' *The Guardian*, 7 June 2015 (https://www.theguardian.com/culture/2015/jun/07/aziz-ansari-comedy-politics-women).

them. His comeback special was directed by Spike Jonze, shot in 16mm black and white with Aziz sitting on a stool, marking his evolution to a more serious comedian.

Self-censorship

External censorship tends to be visible and publicised. But self-censorship is constant. As a comedian, I arrive at a gig early to get a feel for the room – what material are they going for? What's the demographic breakdown? Do they know each other? Are there any problematic audience members? How's the light, do I need to stand forward to be in it? How's the sound, is there pop, is it tinny, do I need to hold the mic away, talk slowly? Do any narratives develop with the other comedian's audience interaction that I need to avoid or can integrate into my act? Has the promoter laid down rules, like no swearing? And during the show, we're constantly assessing the reaction of the room and tailoring our performance.

Self-censorship in this sense is essential, but part of the appeal of comedy is that it plays with acceptability. We have to ensure the show stays within the tolerable boundaries of an audience. Everyone has their own personal idea of what's right and wrong, and how much they'll accept, and how they'll respond to transgressions – and these preferences aren't absolute, they're fluid and contextual. I've had wildly different responses to the same material – from heckles, walkouts, even violence, to people complaining that I didn't go far enough, that I pulled my punches. There's a huge temptation to play safe, to sanitise material in order to mollify potential complainants. Technology has exacerbated this, with Chris Rock telling *New York Magazine* that he has started to censor himself at gigs in case someone is recording him on their phone.[29] Dave Chappelle now takes people's mobile phones and puts them in locked zip bags during his shows.[30]

My own experience

As one of the few openly right-wing comedians, I've fallen foul of censorship – protesters at my shows, reviewers marking me down for my unconscionable opinions, social media storms, venues banning me and promoters blacklisting me. And I've benefited from it too.

I've also performed secret gigs in countries where freedom of speech is severely restricted. In October 2019 I performed an underground show in Brunei, an absolute monarchy with brutal punishments such as stoning, caning and the death penalty for crimes such as blasphemy.[31] These laws are enforced. Government employee Shahiran Shahrani was prosecuted for his 'seditious' Facebook comments about halal certification.[32]

---

29 Comedy in the age of outrage: when jokes go too far. BBC Culture, 4 August 2015 (https://www.bbc.com/culture/article/20150804-comedy-in-the-age -of-outrage-when-jokes-go-too-far).

30 Dave Chappelle, other artists make fans lock phones in pouches during show. *Fox 5*, 11 August 2015 (https://www.fox5dc.com/news/dave-chappelle -other-artists-make-fans-lock-phones-in-pouches-during-show).

31 Brunei's death penalty for blasphemy is 'serious human rights issue'. Humanists UK, 18 September 2019 (https://humanism.org.uk/2019/09/18/ bruneis-death-penalty-for-blasphemy-is-serious-human-rights-breach/).

32 Amnesty International Report 2017/18 Brunei Darussalem (https://www .refworld.org/docid/5a99393a4.html).

As a visiting Westerner, I didn't need to worry too much about getting beheaded for my performance. I was warned not to mention the Sultan, but my material about sex and censorship remained untouched. The illicit nature of the gig added a frisson to the show; the audience were drinking and watching live comedy, two things that are commonplace in the West but banned in Brunei. The risk of military police booting down the door made the performance feel edgy, even though I was essentially shouting dick jokes at middle-aged oil workers – again, psychological reactance defeating the act of censorship.

Most of my shows take place in the West, where I've never experienced this level of censure. But similar to that noticed by Seinfeld and Rock on the college circuit, there is a progressive liberal bias pervasive throughout the comedy and arts community that frequently finds fault with my irreverent, questioning material.

Critiquing my show 'Transgressive' in *Fest*, Lewis Porteous wrote, 'When he complains that it's easier for women to transition than men, he's taking the most loathsome, wrong-headed view possible, on an issue in which it's doubtful he has any personal interest.'

Anyone with a passing knowledge of trans issues knows that it is factually correct to say that transgender men (men who were born with female genitalia) 'pass' more easily than transgender women.[33] This is because small

---

33 Crossing the divide. *The Washington Post*, 20 July 2018 (https://www.wash ingtonpost.com/news/local/wp/2018/07/20/feature/crossing-the-divide -do-men-really-have-it-easier-these-transgender-guys-found-the-truth -was-more-complex/).

feminine men are more common and less noticeable than large masculine women, and markers for maleness such as beards and flat chests are easier to attain than female markers, such as a less pronounced browbone and jawline.

It's anyway a misrepresentation to claim that I have no personal interest in trans issues given that the show in question is about my relationship with a transgender woman. Porteous goes on to castigate 'wilful ignorance on the parts of both performer and audience' – he casts the net of reprobation over people watching the show, too.

The review ends by saying, 'Despite its knuckleheaded ideology, this show could well be one of the funniest shows you see all Fringe, Scotsman Kearse reducing the audience to teary hysterics in a manner recalling no less than Billy Connolly.' A comedy show that's one of the funniest shows of the Fringe might reasonably be expected to get a higher than average score. But Lewis gives me three stars, openly marking me down for my 'knuckleheaded ideology'.

And some of my censors have a significant impact. In 2019 I took my show, 'Right Wing Comedian' to the Perth Fringe in Australia. The show had already caught some flak; while the artistic community proudly champions tolerance and diversity, this isn't extended to political opinions. Other comedians assumed I was either mad or pretending to be right wing to get attention. The idea that a comedian could actually hold mainstream political opinions was unconscionable. I am genuinely right wing. I believe in smaller government, lower taxes, less government interference in people's lives. To woke people, I'm basically Hitler.

So people tried to get me no-platformed. One of the ways this is done is to trawl back through someone's Twitter feed and find something objectionable they posted in 2009 when they were drunk and horny, and use it to whip up an online furore and get that person cancelled, as happened to Kevin Hart when he was announced as an Oscars host.

They did the same thing to me. They went all the way back through my Twitter to ... that afternoon. It was literally the most recent thing I'd posted – a short video from my show, where I spoke about male privilege:

Everyone bangs on about male privilege, but I think it's hard being a man. That's why so many of us are transitioning right now. And you've got to remember, it's way harder for someone like me to transition than it is for a woman. If a woman wants to transition to being a man, in a lot of cases, she just stops shaving. She takes hormones, she grows a beard, and people might say 'I think that man's got tits'. If I want to transition to being a woman, it's a totally different story. I've got to take hormones, undergo extensive surgical procedures to shave down my brow bone and my jaw bone, remove my Adam's apple, put tits in, remove all my body hair, I've got to get a whole new wardrobe of clothes, I could probably keep this shirt, I've got to find high heels in a size 15, learn to walk in them, disguise my male pattern baldness, grow my hair long, learn how to do makeup from YouTube tutorials, talk in a high pitched voice, and at the end of all that expense and effort people are just going to look at me and say 'I think that man's got tits'.

People complained that this material was transphobic. It's not intended to be transphobic. I've got huge respect for transgender people. I think that if you go through all the pain, expense and social stigma of transitioning, you've got more of a right to that gender than I do. I'm just a default gender person – I was born with a penis and I ran with it. If you're transgender, as long as you're not smashing women's powerlifting records with your penis clearly visible through your Lycra, more power to you.

And this material isn't at the expense of transgender people. It's mocking the differing beauty standards of men and women. Men have it easy when it comes to socially approved presentability. A man can sleep in a hedge and wake up looking grizzled and manly, like the late Sean Connery. If a woman sleeps in a hedge, she wakes up looking grizzled and manly, like Sean Connery.

Also I wrote that material with a transgender woman I was dating, because it turns out I was woke before woke people were woke (this was before *Vice* was running articles about it). I totally recommend dating transgender women. At my age, all the women look like Eddie Izzard anyway.

I met Natalia[34] a few years ago and hit it off immediately – as well as being a model she's whip-smart and funny. And she has a formidable inner strength, possibly because of all the obstacles she's overcome, so she doesn't stress about little things.

But a social media mob doesn't ask for context or intent. They saw a white male talking about transgender issues

---

34 Not her real name.

and assumed I must be denigrating transgender people. My show was scheduled for a run at The Court, which is an LGBTQ+ venue. As someone with a transgender girlfriend, it felt appropriate. But others disagreed. The furore kicked off with this post on The Court's Facebook page with a link to the material I wrote with Natalia:

> Why are you hosting this bigoted loser unit's show during Fringeworld? It's a bad look. When you do stuff like this, it shows us that you clearly care more about virtue signalling and profits more than you actually care about our community.

And it snowballed from there. Choice comments in the thread include: 'this is absolutely unacceptable!! THIS GUY IS A TRANSPHOBE!!! You need to sort this out!!!!', 'THIS MAN SHOULD NOT BE WELCOMED INTO OUR SAFE FOR QUEER PEOPLE SPACES SHAME ON YOU THE COURT'.

Someone posted a link to an article where I discuss having a transgender girlfriend, giving context to the offending material, but it was deleted after the person posting it was attacked online.

The Court responded: 'Thanks so much for bringing this to our attention. We have cancelled this show. We do apologise if we have offended anyone.' I fully understand and support their decision – their venue should be a place where LGBTQ+ people can feel safe. I didn't want to jeopardise this.

The immediate consequence for me was that I had to spend AU$3,500 hiring a new venue that wasn't as nice or as central as The Court. And I experienced some anguish – I didn't mean to upset anyone like this, I felt that my material had been misunderstood, that people who would enjoy the show had been put off from seeing it. I worried that the promoter who'd programmed my show would lose the venue and other comedians would be affected.

But in the end, my show was a financial success at the new venue, helped by my new-found notoriety which led to media coverage and a boost in ticket sales. An excerpt from my show went viral on YouTube.

In defence of censors

Does this mean I think that censorship is always unnecessary and counterproductive? No. In policing there's the 'broken windows theory'[35] – that seemingly minor misdeeds such as graffiti and broken windows create an environment where potential criminals feel that crime can be committed. Similarly, speech can normalise behaviours. Comedians have to be mindful that our words can have real-life consequences. The racism of comedians in the 1970s legitimised racist attitudes, and their no-platforming contributed to the UK becoming a better, more tolerant place.

More recently, when Jo Brand joked on BBC radio that people should throw acid at politicians instead of milkshakes, she did so against a backdrop of increasing rancour in British politics, with politicians subject to physical attacks, sometimes fatal as in the tragic case of Jo Cox, and

---

35 Originated by George Kelling and James Q. Wilson (1982).

acid attacks increasing across the UK. It's conceivable that someone could have committed an acid attack against a politician, and her comment would have helped make the environment more conducive to this crime.

She was investigated by the broadcasting watchdog Ofcom, but no action was taken.[36] In fairness, her joke clearly worked in the room, and comedians should feel free to cross the line without fear of retribution – you've got to crash the car to find out how fast it can go. The fault lay more with the editor who allowed the quip to be broadcast.

And when comedians target a specific person, as Louise Reay did when she identified her estranged husband in her comedy show, they shouldn't be immune to defamation laws. The law allows comedians to defend themselves if they're in the right.

The impact of censorship

The impact of censorship ripples on through self-censorship. Few would dare publish a cartoon of the Prophet Muhammad following the *Charlie Hebdo* massacre, or take to the stage in Brunei to mock the Sultan. Fearful of being accused of hate speech, comedians in the West tread carefully when satirising woke culture.

However, psychological reactance often subverts the aim of the censors, as the act of banning something makes it attractive. My underground show in Brunei was elevated

36 Jo Brand to face no further action over battery acid joke. *The Guardian*, 27 January 2020 (https://www.theguardian.com/culture/2020/jan/27/jo -brand-face-no-further-action-battery-acid-joke).

above the mundane by the frisson of illegality. The massacre of *Charlie Hebdo* staff led to far more people seeing their cartoons of the Prophet Muhammad, and a huge boost in sales. Removing much-loved TV shows plays into the hands of the far right, who use it to assert that white culture is under threat.

When comedians such as Owen Benjamin are banned from social media, they take their fans with them to alternative platforms that don't filter prejudiced content, which is surely less healthy. And Mark Meechan's harassment and censorship has by his own admission pushed the former leftist to the right, with him becoming a UKIP candidate in 2019.

Censoring comedians seems largely unnecessary and self-defeating. We're already self-censoring; when we perform we're constantly judged by a jury of people who let us know if we say anything unacceptable. They're called 'the audience'.

And confrontational, offensive comedy can have noble intentions. Chris Rock's seminal routine 'black people are more racist than white people' is offensive at face value. But in context it's socially progressive, breaking down stereotypes about black people and revealing the strata in society – showing the commonalities in a way that the bland simplistic niceties of a traditional anti-racism campaign don't do. Similarly, Lenny Bruce's censored material made people think about the racist language they used.

Some think that even the tawdry racists of the 1970s may have had value. In his book *Seriously Funny*, Howard Jacobson (1997) makes the case for offensive comedy being an important safety valve on society, with Bernard Manning's racist jokes 'lancing the boil'. He goes on to say that as a Jew, he's 'far more threatened by those who would wipe out ethnic jokes than by those who unthinkingly make them'.

And as comedians have become more like politicians, self-censoring to ensure they don't offend anyone, so politicians have become more like comedians. Donald Trump has an innate reflexive stand-up sensibility – he says the most outrageous, hilarious, cruel things, appealing to the basest places in people's hearts. The world might be a better place with dignified politicians and scandalous comedians.

All truly progressive ideas are offensive. When Galileo proposed that the Earth orbited the Sun he was condemned as a heretic. The Civil Rights movement was essential but it was hugely offensive to many, as were women's rights, LGBTQ rights and disability rights. We can't ever assume that the prevailing wisdom is beyond criticism; and we can't assume that the people who police our speech will act fairly. A healthy society allows tolerance of ideas and diversity of opinions. And a comedy club is an ideal forum to do just that.

7 WHY FREE SPEECH IN ADVERTISING MATTERS

J. R. Shackleton

In the more than a century and a half since modern advertising techniques and agencies began, advertising has become ubiquitous, and a major economic[1] and social influence on our lives.

In nineteenth-century Britain the only legal constraints on what has been called 'commercial speech' – then mainly in the form of posters, billboards and newspaper advertisements – were those, such as the law on defamation, which also covered other forms of communication. Otherwise, *caveat emptor*.

In the twentieth century, however, concerns about risks to public safety from dangerous products, and belief in the need to protect people from misleading claims, produced specific legislation concerning the advertising of particular products (medicines and tobacco are important

---

1 The UK spent over £22 billion in 2019 on advertising and the industry also generated £8 billion of exports, making it our second largest service exporter. The industry employs about half a million people in the UK; it provides 1/3 of television revenue, 2/3 of press revenue, and sponsors large numbers of social, cultural and sporting institutions.

examples). There are also some restrictions on location of advertisements in public places.[2] Wider concerns, however, crystallised into a system of self-regulation.

Initially, this system focused on relatively uncontentious issues raised by consumer complaints, but in recent years advertising regulation has become much more proactive. It has inevitably had to widen its scope as a result of the explosion of new forms of digital advertising,[3] including the role of 'influencers'. But it has also developed ambitions to regulate over more and more subjects.

Critics charge firstly, that it has become a key component in the ever-growing reach of the nanny state and, secondly, has given itself a worrying new role in social engineering, attempting to reshape cultural and social attitudes to gender issues and the family. It may also be a portent of much tighter restrictions to come, which will threaten wider notions of free speech.

'Good' and 'bad' advertising?

Attitudes to advertising have always been ambivalent. They have been characterised by a never-ending search for a distinction between 'good' and 'bad' advertising. Thorstein Veblen in his *The Theory of the Leisure Class* (1899)

---

2   Dating back to the Advertisement Regulation Act 1907, which allowed local authorities to restrict advertising in parks and beauty spots.

3   Between 2005 and 2016, the proportion of advertising spend on print fell from 39 per cent to 11 per cent while the proportion on digital advertising rose from 8 per cent to 48 per cent. The third main area of spend, TV advertising, remained constant at around 23 per cent, although it was now spread over many more channels (House of Lords 2018: 10).

saw advertising as the source of wasteful 'conspicuous consumption' while at the same time as being a necessary element in the capitalist system. Around the same time the great economist Alfred Marshall tried to distinguish between 'constructive' advertising and 'combative' advertising. Constructive advertising makes people aware of opportunities for buying and selling which they would not otherwise know about, and thus serves a useful purpose. Combative advertising, on the other hand, is designed to push brand names and lock consumers into habitual purchases; Marshall thought it tends to reduce competition and raise prices (Liebhafsky 1993: 77).

Half a century later Nicholas Kaldor (1950) produced an influential critique of advertising which, while recognising that it might stimulate investment and innovation, and usefully boost consumption in recessions, nevertheless saw it as wasteful (consuming more resources than necessary to carry out its informational role) and as tending to increase industrial concentration.

By the 1950s, the concerns of economists were augmented by journalists and social critics such as Vance Packard, whose *The Hidden Persuaders* (1957) criticised advertisers' use of motivational and other psychological research to manipulate consumers. Although overblown, his critique was influential in creating a climate where some regulation was considered reasonable.

In the US, however, the First Amendment[4] protects the right to free speech in the press, the public square and

---

4   See Epstein (1987) for a discussion of the First Amendment's implications for free speech.

nowadays in electronic media – and there is a strong argument, recognised in several legal cases, that commercial free speech – advertising – is also entitled to protection (Redish 2017). In a celebrated judgement, for example, the Supreme Court held that a state cannot limit pharmacists' right to advertise drug prices.[5] Advertisers, though still subject to many constraints, are consequently rather freer than those in the UK.

The economic argument for free speech in the marketplace was developed by Ronald Coase (1974).[6] He pointed out that, while it is widely accepted that governments are competent to regulate product markets where there are believed to be market failures (such as consumer ignorance, externalities or fear of monopolies), few accept that intervention in the 'market for ideas' should be treated on the same basis. While moral, religious and political ideas may similarly generate externalities, prey on other people's ignorance and so forth, liberal democracies do not approve of bans and restrictions. Attachment to this type of intellectual free speech is 'the only area where laissez-faire is still respectable', Coase noted (ibid.: 385), quoting Aaron Director, Milton Friedman's brother-in-law.

The paradox is that government intervention, believed harmful in the market for ideas, is seen as beneficial, even imperative, in the market for goods and services. Coase explains this by the self-interest and self-esteem

---

5 *Virginia State Pharmacy Board v. Virginia Citizens Consumer Council*, 425 U.S. 748 (1976).

6 Although his ideas were developed much earlier, in an unpublished 1957 lecture (Harris and Seldon 2014: 99).

of intellectuals. Others must be regulated, but regulation should not apply to journalists, academics, clerics or politicians. He quotes Milton's *Areopagitica* as the archetype of intellectual disdain for 'licensers' or censors: the sort of people who want to do such a job are likely to be 'ignorant, imperious, and remiss, or basely pecuniary' (Coase 1974: 388–89). Coase's view, however, was that

> I do not believe that this distinction between the market for goods and the market for ideas is valid. There is no fundamental difference ... and in deciding on public policy with regard to them, we need to take into account the same considerations. In all markets, producers have some reasons for being honest and some for being dishonest; consumers have some information but are not fully informed or even able to digest the information they have; regulators commonly wish to do a good job but are often incompetent and subject to the influence of special interests, because, like all of us, they are human beings whose strongest motives are not the highest.

We probably shouldn't apply the same rules for each individual market, Coase argues, but should certainly apply a similar cost–benefit calculus to determine appropriate rules. Doing so, he argues provocatively, we could say that 'the case for government intervention in the market of ideas is much stronger than it is, in general, for the market for goods' (ibid.).

For example, the externalities produced by ideas are likely to be considerable, for good or ill. Is this evidence of 'market failure', requiring state intervention? Or take consumer ignorance (which economists more politely term 'asymmetric information'): more people are probably capable of choosing between different breakfast cereals or brands of washing-up liquid than are able to evaluate economic and social policy. Yet we regulate the images which can appear on cereal packets but not (at least yet, see later) the content of party manifestos or economics textbooks.

Coase concludes his 1974 article by saying that we must form a judgement on the competence (and beneficence) of government. If we think it is beyond reproach, it should intervene much more in the market for ideas; if it is very incompetent and venal, it should intervene much less in the market for goods.

This tongue-in-cheek conclusion was, predictably, misunderstood by Coase's critics. They took it to mean that he was in favour of increased government regulation of intellectual free speech. In a later and more substantial article drawing on numerous cases and legal judgements, Coase (1977) spelt out his argument unambiguously. He wanted less regulation all round.

One of the interesting points made in this second article is Coase's criticism of the distinction between 'good' information and 'bad' persuasion[7] (Coase 1977: 9):

---

7   A point well made by Ralph Harris and Arthur Seldon (2014), who note that even the apparently 'pure' information provided by a train timetable is intended to persuade people to travel, while persuasive advertising may lead people to try a product and thus gain more information about its characteristics.

> Persuasive advertising, which conveys no information about the properties of the goods and services being advertised but achieves its effect through an emotional appeal, is commonly disapproved of ... It is not clear why. Any advertisement which induces people to consume a product conveys information, since the act of consumption gives more information about the properties of a product or service than could be done by the advertisement itself. Persuasive advertising is thus also informative ... Advertising of new products, I suspect, normally informs ... through inducing the consumer to try the product and thus informing him in the most direct way.

Coase also draws attention to the pragmatic benefits of advertising. Rather than promoting monopoly, as Kaldor and others argued, advertising can often lead to greater competition and lower prices. He quotes Lee Benham's well-known empirical examination of the effect of advertising bans on the price of eyeglasses and the services of opticians: Benham (1972) found that the average price of spectacles in US states which forbade optometrists to advertise was 25 per cent higher than in states where they were allowed to do so.[8]

But it is not just price information which benefits consumers and boosts competition. As the philosopher John Gray (1992: 4–5) points out:

---

[8] Other studies examining advertising of breakfast cereals (Clark 2007) and drugs (Cady 1976) have found similar effects.

the indispensable complement to market pricing is provided by advertising, which focuses on the qualities of the product itself. Indeed, in the absence of advertising, the consumer would inevitably remain ignorant, not only of many of the features of specific products, but also (and perhaps even more significantly) of the range of products that are available.

Advertising regulation in the UK

Regulation of advertising in the UK is not as easy to understand as it might be. There are some statutory restrictions (for instance, on the advertising and labelling of medicines,[9] food, tobacco and alcohol). Devolved administrations and local authorities have some (surprisingly arbitrary) powers to ban display adverts of which they disapprove.[10]

But regulation of most commercial speech is in principle in the hands of the advertising industry itself – albeit,

---

9 There are rules for advertising laid down by the Medicines and Healthcare Products Regulatory Agency, an executive agency of the Department of Health, which pre-screens adverts for a fee (see https://www.gov.uk/gov ernment/organisations/medicines-and-healthcare-products-regulatory -agency/about).

10 Transport for London, for example, has in recent years banned adverts featuring 'beach-ready bodies' (https://www.theguardian.com/media/2016/ jun/13/sadiq-khan-moves-to-ban-body-shaming-ads-from-london-tran sport) and so-called 'junk food' adverts (https://www.bbc.co.uk/news/uk -england-london-47318803). Edinburgh City Council has banned street advertising boards (https://www.rnib.org.uk/scotland-scotland-news-and -media/scotland's-towns-and-cities-should-follow-edinburgh's-lead-and -ban).

as we shall see, with some statutory back-up. How did this come about?

When commercial television began broadcasting in 1955, this was the first time that advertising was made subject to any general formal regulation. Under the Act empowering the Independent Television Authority to set up commercial television in Britain, programme contractors were forbidden to show religious or political advertisements (though they were required to provide a certain amount of religious programming, and to carry party political broadcasts) and made responsible for the content of adverts[11] in the same way as they were responsible for programme content (Fletcher 2008). They had to set up an Advertising Advisory Committee to draw up a set of principles for advertisers, involving 'good taste and propriety'.

The regulation of television advertising raised the issue of regulating other forms of commercial speech. Thus in 1961, the Advertising Association and other interested parties proposed that advertisements in non-broadcast media (such as newspapers, magazines, posters, direct mailings or billboards) should be subject to self-regulation rather than government intervention.[12]

---

11 This requirement led contractors to set up a system of pre-screening commercials, which continues to the present day. It is now run by Clearcast, a body funded by ITV, Channel 4, Sky and Warner Media.

12 This may well have been motivated by fear that the Molony Committee on Consumer Protection, sitting at the time, would impose statutory regulation. In the event, the Committee gave its blessing to the proposed new initiative, concluding that self-regulation 'should be given a chance to prove itself' (quoted in Ramsay (2006: 68)).

As a result, agencies, media and advertisers formed the Committee of Advertising Practice (CAP)[13] and produced the first edition of the British Code of Advertising Practice. In 1962 the CAP established the Advertising Standards Authority (ASA) as the independent regulator under this Code. At first funded on an ad hoc basis, in the 1970s the ASA began to receive an annual levy of 0.1 per cent on advertising space costs.[14] In 1988 the Control of Misleading Advertisement Regulations gave the ASA's decisions some limited legal support[15] as it could refer persistently uncooperative advertisers to the Office of Fair Trading. Changes in government regulations and institutions since then have passed this legal back-up to Trading Standards. It is rarely used, as advertisers almost always end up conforming to ASA judgements.

This century, the ASA's scope has increased considerably. In 2004 the ASA/CAP system assumed responsibility for TV and radio advertisements, contracted out from Ofcom (which had inherited responsibility from earlier broadcast regulators). This created what the ASA refers to as a 'one-stop shop' for advertising complaints. A new

13 Now the UK Code of Non-broadcast Advertising and Direct and Promotional Marketing, the 12th edition of which runs to over a hundred pages (https://www.asa.org.uk/uploads/assets/47eb51e7-028d-4509-ab3c0f4822 c9a3c4/The-Cap-code.pdf).

14 An Advertising Standards Board of Finance, independent from the ASA, collects the levy.

15 In relation to advertisements that are misleading, rather than the wider brief that the ASA now has. The narrow scope of this back-up was because it was in response to the EU Directive on Misleading Advertising (Ramsay 2006: 68).

committee, the Broadcast Committee of Advertising Practice, was set up to write and maintain the Broadcasting Advertising Code.

In 2009 the ASA's powers were extended to cover video-on-demand, a growing format which has increasingly replaced traditional broadcast television. It had already had powers, from 1995 onwards, to cover paid-for space online (banner ads and sponsored search); in 2010 the CAP extended the ASA's remit to cover claims made on companies' own websites and advertisements and endorsements on social networking sites.

When the ASA starts an investigation of a complaint, it asks the advertiser for comments and justification. Once the investigation is completed, a draft recommendation is sent to the advertiser and complainant(s) for comments. The draft is then sent to the ASA Council, which discusses the complaint and the draft recommendation and reaches a conclusion. The full adjudication is then posted on the ASA's website and is publicised in the media. There are facilities for a time-limited appeal to an Independent Reviewer[16] if new evidence is forthcoming, or if there is some flaw in the investigation or adjudication.

If a complaint is upheld, the ASA can demand an ad campaign be amended or withdrawn. It can require future campaigns to be pre-vetted. But these powers are by consent: there is little legal basis for them. If an advertiser refused to play ball, there's not much the ASA could do. In

---

16 Imposed following a court ruling that ASA decisions were subject to judicial review.

principle companies could just brazen it out, confident that the grounds under which Trading Standards could intervene are limited. But of course companies worried about reputational damage usually acquiesce (with varying degrees of grace)[17] and withdraw the relevant campaign. This often means that they incur considerable costs.

Self-regulation has certain advantages, being able to draw upon expertise which might not be available to a government regulator and often able to negotiate and compromise in a way which a legally constrained body could not. But it does mean that self-regulators are typically subject to less scrutiny than if rule-making was the responsibility of a public body.

Moreover, independent self-regulatory bodies (such as charities and the innumerable quangos which administer great swathes of publicly financed business in the UK) arguably attract certain types of individual to work for them. Such employees may often have their own agendas and develop new objectives and projects with few external constraints on their behaviour – a form of 'regulatory capture' which is often overlooked.[18]

---

17 The ASA has repeatedly upheld complaints against Ryanair, whose CEO Michael O'Leary has made clear his distaste for their judgement, while ultimately accepting them. On one occasion he described the ASA as a 'bunch of complete idiots' (https://www.managementtoday.co.uk/michael-oleary-asa-bunch-complete-idiots/article/1119915).

18 The theory of economic regulation (Stigler 1971) tends to focus on the effects of industry interests coming to dominate regulators. While this certainly happens, a clique of professional regulators, flitting from one body to another, has grown up in the UK.

Advertising and the curtailment of free speech

Coverage of new media is not the only extension of ASA regulatory powers and influence in recent years. Its role is now very different from that when it began.

When the ASA was set up, it aimed to ensure advertising was 'legal, decent, honest and truthful'. This seems at first glance unexceptionable, although a classical liberal could find it problematic. John Gray (1992: 9), for instance, objects to advertising rules which

> transfer the responsibility for making an assessment of the risks from the responsible individual to the state. Implicitly, they thereby deny the capacity of the individual to make a reasonable evaluation of the relevant risks on the basis of the information that unrestricted expression would make available. This is an implication with far reaching consequences for freedom of expression in other, non-commercial spheres of social life.

Of these original aims, ensuring legality is reasonably clearcut, although it might be argued that laws against fraud and defamation make separate regulation unnecessary. Decency, honesty and truthfulness are virtues to which we may all aspire, but their correlates are contestable: opinions may differ. And rules are applied far more strictly in commercial speech than in other forms of discourse.

For example, in films, the theatre, TV drama, social media and the press it is still just about possible for an individual to make a legal, decent, honest and truthful statement such as 'I enjoy smoking cigarettes'. This can't be done in an advertisement. In films and the theatre, since the abolition of the Lord Chamberlain and relaxation of film certification, actors can swear or take their clothes off and simulate sexual intercourse. They can't do so in an advertisement.[19] Politicians can make speeches or give interviews which are economical with the truth – although more of this later – while any factual statement in an advertisement must be verifiable.

The ASA now interprets its brief very differently from in the past. In its most recent Annual Report (2019) this is spelt out: 'We work to make ads responsible. We do this by taking action against misleading, harmful or offensive advertising and ensuring compliance.'

In the 1960s, complaints were arriving at a rate of around 300 in a full year, mostly about misleading offers, mail order goods which failed to arrive, the accuracy of pricing and similar problems. Only a handful (3 out of 244 in a nine-month period in 1967) seem to have been about matters of taste and appropriateness of adverts. The ASA was essentially reactive, though there was some monitoring of newspapers and magazines.

By contrast there were 34,717 complaints in 2019 about 24,886 advertisements. While the majority of complaints were still about advertisements which were misleading, many were now about 'harm' (very broadly defined) or offensiveness.

---

19 It could be said that people voluntarily choose to watch controversial films, plays and TV programmes, while they do not choose to be exposed to all types of advert. This might argue for some difference in the rules although – as in the Missguided swimwear example discussed later – this is not necessarily justified.

This was particularly true in respect of broadcast advertisements, where 3,549 complaints were about offensiveness `and 2,405 about harm, considerably outnumbering the 3,179 complaints about commercials which are misleading.

Another difference from the early years is the ASA's own actions to enforce its rules. Rather than simply responding to complaints, it investigates on its own account: in 2019 it resolved 4,469 'own-initiative compliance cases'. The techniques employed are often innovative. One might be seen as a form of entrapment: using avatars (which mimic the online profiles of child Internet users) to identify likely exposure of children to online advertisements for high fat, salt or sugar (HFSS) food and drinks (ASA/CAP 2020: 10).

The technique is also being used to track Botox adverts on Instagram, and other projects are planned to monitor whether children are exposed to age-restricted ads, including alcohol and gambling, as well as HFSS products.

These examples show how the ASA and CAP now have an agenda going far beyond preventing misleading or dishonest advertising. It is part of a wider project (promoted strongly since 2013 by Public Health England and similar bodies in other parts of the UK) which uncritically accepts that the state has a responsibility to prevent or reduce 'harms' to the population, rather than leave that responsibility to individuals and their families.

'Harms'

Harms were at first associated with health. The process began with tobacco. In 1965 cigarette advertising on television was banned. In 1990 cigars and loose tobacco followed. From 2003 press advertisements and billboards were banned; from 2005 sports sponsorship. The last ten years have seen the end of vending machines and displays in shops; most recently, plain packaging has been mandated.

Prolonged use of tobacco carries known health risks. Classical liberals (Gray 1992: 16) may argue that this alone cannot justify a complete ban on advertising tobacco products: 'it may be that a life ruled by a passion for prudence … is a lesser form of life than one in which … we take our chances'. Snowdon (2017: 158), more pragmatically, points out that advertising bans make it impossible for companies to market safer tobacco products.

Be that as it may, as the 'harms' agenda has widened, the risks become less obvious and the argument for restrictions more tenuous. Alcohol is probably next in line in terms of perceived damage to health, although relatively few users of alcohol suffer life-threatening illness as a consequence.

Rules applying across all media forbid alcohol advertising which may appeal to young people (such as cartoons) or reflect youth culture. Any individuals featuring in advertisements must appear to be over the age of 25 (even though drinking is legal at 18). More generally, nothing in adverts must give the impression that alcohol boosts confidence, increases popularity, is associated with sporting success or sexual prowess.

A still further remove from direct damage to health is the emphasis on HFSS food and drink, which in moderate quantities will harm very few people, but which is seen as contributing to obesity and possibly implicated in heart disease and other ailments. The government has recently reacted to the overweight prime minister's brush with Covid-19 death by proposing substantial new curbs on advertising.[20]

Since 2007, there has been a prohibition on scheduling HFSS advertising around programming commissioned for or likely to appeal particularly to children. To determine whether a programme is likely to appeal particularly to children, broadcasters rely on 'audience indexing' in which audience data are used to determine which programmes would attract a high percentage of children compared to the total audience watching; the 'particular appeal' prohibition applies throughout the broadcast day, including after 9 p.m.

As children now view a great deal of YouTube and other Internet content, restrictions have since 2017 also been imposed on online HFSS advertising. It is now proposed that no TV adverts for HFSS products should be permitted before the 9 p.m. watershed, and that no online advertising for these foodstuffs should be permitted at all. The first of these restrictions can be imposed virtually overnight by Ofcom fiat, but restrictions on Internet advertising will require legislation.

---

20 A consultation was launched in November 2020 on a government proposal to ban all online adverts for foods high in fat, sugar and salt 'to tackle the obesity crisis and get the nation fit and healthy'. New public consultation on total ban of online advertising for unhealthy foods (www.gov.uk).

HFSS foods are often carelessly described in the media as 'junk food' – with cakes, burgers, crisps, fizzy drinks and chocolate coming to mind. However, as critics[21] of these restrictions have pointed out, the definition is based on nutritional profiles which also include many products which are normally considered part of a balanced diet – eggs, raisins and sultanas, tinned fruit, orange juice, most yoghurts, cheese, butter, ham, tomato soup, certain types of bread. A farm delivery business, for example, recently fell foul of Transport for London's interpretation of advertising restrictions.[22]

Another area where advertising is regulated under specific rules to reduce harm is gambling. The Committee on Advertising Practice, the Broadcast Committee of Advertising Practice and the Advertising Standards Authority are supplemented by the Gambling Industry Code for Socially Responsible Advertising Practice. Although gambling does not pose direct threats to people's health, these codes assert that some people's gambling behaviour 'could lead to financial, social or emotional harm' and 'exploit the susceptibilities, aspirations, credulity, lack of knowledge of children, young persons or other vulnerable persons'.[23]

---

21 What is junk food? IEA Briefing March 2019 (https://iea.org.uk/wp-con tent/uploads/2019/03/IEA_Briefing_March2019_approval.pdf).

22 Can you spot the junk food in this ad? TfL could. Farmdrop, 1 March 2019 (https://www.farmdrop.com/blog/the-contradictions-in-tfls-junk-food -advertising-ban/).

23 Advertising codes quoted in Woodhouse (2020).

These concerns lead to frequent interventions. In April 2018 CAP 'guidance'[24] restricted adverts creating artificial urgency ('Bet now!') and emphasising monetary gains from gambling. In April 2019 restrictions[25] came into force on the use of celebrities, licensed characters from movies and TV, sportspeople, animated characters, and anybody appearing to be under 25. The prime intention was to protect under-18s, although there is little evidence of underage gambling or that children are significantly affected by gambling advertisements. In April 2020 the Betting and Gaming Council voluntarily introduced further restrictions on advertising during the Covid-19 pandemic.[26]

The list of potential 'harms' which could be claimed to justify advertising restrictions can be extended indefinitely. One area where we can expect pressure for bans in the future is products which may be implicated in climate change. For example, environmental activists have called for a ban on advertising sports utility vehicles (SUVs),[27] which generate more greenhouse gases than other vehicles.

---

24 Advertising Standards Authority: 'Gambling Advertising: responsibility and problem gambling' (https://www.asa.org.uk/uploads/assets/upload ed/9d0bca96-290b-4fad-9ba33df7103a3fa9.pdf).

25 Committees of Advertising Practice: 'Regulatory Statement: gambling advertising guidance. Protecting children and young people', 13 February 2019 (https://www.asa.org.uk/uploads/assets/uploaded/43072c78-8a0e-4 345-ab21b8cbb8af7432.pdf).

26 Betting and Gaming Council: '10 Pledge Action Plan announced' (https:// bettingandgamingcouncil.com/news/10pledges-safergambling/).

27 Ban SUV adverts to meet UK climate goals, report urges. *The Guardian*, 3 August 2020 (https://www.theguardian.com/environment/2020/aug/03/ ban-suv-adverts-to-meet-uk-climate-goals-report-urges).

But this is only a matter of degree: a successful ban on advertising SUVs would surely be followed by demands for a ban on all fossil-fuel vehicles.

'Offence'

These 'harm' issues, although contested by classical liberals, are one thing. Even more worrying, I would argue, are issues concerning 'offence'. Section 4.2 of the BCAP code[28] states that

> Advertisements must not cause serious or widespread offence against generally accepted moral, social or cultural standards. Particular care must be taken to avoid causing offence on the grounds of: age; disability; gender; gender reassignment; marriage and civil partnership; pregnancy and maternity; race; religion or belief; sex; and sexual orientation.

The problem is that advertising regulators have taken it upon themselves to define what those 'moral, social or cultural standards' are, or, perhaps more accurately, what they *ought* to be. In 2017 the ASA and CAP published *Deceptions, Perceptions and Harms: A Report on Gender Stereotypes in Advertising*, which called for 'a tougher line' on advertisements which could be held to feature 'stereotypical gender roles and characteristics'.

---

28 The BCAP code: the UK code of broadcasting advertising (https://www.asa
.org.uk/uploads/assets/846f25eb-f474-47c1-ab3ff571e3db5910/2828d080
-b29f-4b6c-8de66fbc7a6cd1f8/BCAP-Code-full.pdf).

This report was based on academic research (often qualitative research, from a critical perspective drawing on media theory), submissions from interested parties,[29] consultations and seminars.

It was asserted that stereotypes can be offensive to large numbers of people, and the ASA and CAP thought this particularly important. Interestingly, however, the report notes that offence can sometimes be vicarious: 'whilst participants often claimed not to feel personally offended by an advert, they did express offence on behalf of other groups in society' (p. 59). This is classic paternalism.

Several participants in seminars held to discuss the issue argued for maintaining freedom of speech in this area. These arguments were countered with the formula that free speech and liberty to offend do not give a right to cause harm. A riposte to this increasingly heard dismissal of free speech is that harms surely need to be obvious and serious to begin to justify restrictions. What are these harms?

It was argued that gender stereotypes have the potential to cause 'mental, physical or social harm'. But evidence on this was tenuous. The report endorsed (p. 42), for example, claims that high male suicide rates arise partly because men are upset at being unable to live up to cultural expectations of masculinity. And it was suggested that there might be a loss to the economy of £150 billion because stereotypes help maintain the gender pay gap (p. 25) and

---

29 Including pressure groups such as Stonewall, the Women's Equality Party and the Fawcett Society (which the ASA report's coordinator Ella Smillie later joined).

therefore lead to slower economic growth, a claim which to economists is debatable, to say the least.

As for the view that much stereotyping in advertising[30] is meant to be ironic and humorous, the report sternly argued that research (see, for example, Ford et al. 2008) suggested that exposure to sexist humour is linked to increased prejudice and sexist views. So that was that.

Overall, four broad areas of potential harm were listed in the report (pp. 58–59), to be avoided in future: focus on perfect bodies, 'gratuitous and unnecessary sexualisation', stereotypical gender roles and the perpetuation of these stereotypes over time.

These were to be the basis for new guidance to advertisers. Following consultations about the precise wording of new guidelines, the policy[31] came into force in June 2019. The guidelines include examples of now-forbidden scenarios, such as a woman being apparently solely responsible for cleaning, a man looking like an idiot if he tries to carry out a stereotypically female role, or a new mother trying to maintain her make-up and keeping the house tidy rather than prioritising her own emotional wellbeing.

Quite a few adverts have failed to meet the new criteria. An early ASA ban was imposed on one involving two new fathers who chat about Philadelphia cheese while

---

30 Arguably, stereotyping of some sort is essential to adverts, which have to tell a story in a short period of time.

31 Ban on harmful gender stereotypes in ads comes into force. CAP News, 14 June 2019 (https://www.asa.org.uk/news/ban-on-harmful-gender-ste reotypes-in-ads-comes-into-force.html).

a child disappears on a conveyor belt[32]; another was the Vauxhall advert showing a new mother calmly sitting on a bench alongside a pushchair while men (and one woman) engaged in various acts of derring-do.[33] Of course, neither of these brief scenarios could have been banned were they part of a comedy show or a documentary.

A number of such delinquencies involve sexual imagery. While it is perhaps understandable that some people might complain about inappropriate imagery, it seems that the rules can be interpreted regardless of context. Take for instance the judgement against Missguided swimwear, a provocative ad for which appeared in a break during *Love Island*. The ASA ruled:

> we acknowledged that there were similarities between the content of the ad and the programme, which was a reality dating show in which male and female contestants were featured often wearing swimwear or other revealing clothing and sometimes engaging in degrees of sexual behaviour. However, we considered that some viewers who enjoyed the programme would nevertheless be seriously offended by advertising that presented women as sexual objects. Because the ad objectified

---

32 Philadelphia advert first to be banned under gender stereotype rules for suggesting men 'can't care for children'. *Evening Standard*, 13 August 2019 (https://www.standard.co.uk/news/uk/philadelphia-cheese-advert-ban ned-over-claims-it-suggests-men-unable-to-care-for-children-a4212621 .html).

33 ASA ruling on Volkswagen Group UK Ltd, 14 August 2019 (https://www .asa.org.uk/rulings/volkswagen-group-uk-ltd-g19-1023922.html).

women, we concluded that it was irresponsible and likely to cause serious offence.

This verdict offers a particularly clear example of the way in which there is greater freedom in developing television content than there is in television advertising. We are asked seriously to believe that somebody who watched this programme – the major appeal of which is to young people who enjoy watching semi-naked young men and women pairing off for sex – would be offended by an advert aimed at a similar demographic. I very much doubt such a person exists[34] – there was apparently only one complaint, and understandable anonymity rules prevent us from knowing whether this was a genuinely offended individual or a person or organisation wishing to make a political point in the increasingly fractious culture wars. It seems absurd that if one person finds something – anything – offensive it can lead to a ban.

The decision appears even more difficult to defend when we consider that the advert had, like the Philadelphia and Volkswagen ads, been approved by Clearcast, the organisation which approves scripts and final versions of adverts in advance of their being shown, for showing after 9 p.m.

Clearcast (owned by ITV, Channel 4, Sky and Warner Media) takes considerable care in its pre-approval process, yet frequently finds itself on the wrong end of ASA

---

34 In their response to the ASA, ITV said that 'the ad depicted similar values, swimwear and scenes as *Love Island* and that they were surprised to learn that a viewer of the programme had considered the content of the ad offensive'.

adjudications. This 'double jeopardy' is a feature of advertising regulation; agencies go through an elaborate and costly process of drafts and amendments following Clearcast comments, but this does not seem to offer much protection. In the Missguided case Clearcast told the ASA that

> because the ad was promoting a swimwear range, the body of the models would always be exposed and while some of the poses did have a sexual tone, they did not consider them to be overly sexualised. They said the ad was aimed at women to whom the imagery and clothing would appeal, rather than that its intention or portrayal was to objectify women and that the scheduling within *Love Island* was appropriate because of the shared themes and imagery.

It is clear, therefore, that there can be legitimate differences of opinion over the meaning of words such as 'offensive' and 'objectification'. This suggests that there should be much higher barriers to the imposition of bans than is currently the case.

A big part of the problem is that the decisions on complaints are made by the ASA Council, a thirteen-member body made up of people who are unrepresentative of the population. So far as can be seen from their brief biographies[35] they are all highly educated. A third of them work in

---

35 Available at https://www.asa.org.uk/about-asa-and-cap/people/asa-coun cil.html.

the advertising industry, although none appear currently to be 'creatives'. Most of the rest work or have worked in in quangos and charities such as the Financial Services Authority, the British Board of Film Classification, the Mayor's Office, the Consumer Council for Northern Ireland, and the Scottish Legal Complaints Commission. Council members are 'diverse' in that an appropriate proportion are drawn from ethnic minorities. But none of them seem to be the part of the demographic which enjoys *Love Island*, nor indeed of the wider population of television viewers and media consumers.

The new powers of the ASA in relation to gender issues are unlikely to be its only incursion into manipulating and directing public discourse. It already has policies towards representation of ethnicity, which have greatly increased, sometimes possibly disproportionately, the representation of visible minorities; in light of the current concern over Black Lives Matter, it seems inevitable that advocacy groups will demand that the ASA tighten rules in this area too.

Perhaps most worryingly, the ASA has itself already come out with an astonishing demand that political advertising be regulated (ASA/CAP 2020: 10):

Why can political parties act with apparent impunity when making claims in ads and other election materials? To many, including those in ad land, it doesn't make sense that ads for commercial products by businesses large and small throughout the UK should be held to greater account than ads that might swing votes and flip seats. We at the ASA agree. That's why we're stating clearly that we think claims in political advertising should be regulated.

Interestingly, the ASA is here repeating Ronald Coase's argument, but flipping it the other way round. While Coase argued that commercial speech should be liberalised and treated in the same way as political speech, the regulator is saying that political speech should be subject to greater strictures in line with the way we treat advertising.

Although the ASA's Chief Executive is not sufficiently arrogant to demand these regulatory powers for the ASA itself, he generously stands ready to share its experience and 'to contribute our expertise to a more collaborative regulatory arrangement', whatever that means. The prospects of people such as the ASA's council – whose voting intentions are unlikely ever to mirror those of the electorate – adjudicating what can and cannot be said in party manifestos is one which should surely fill us with dread.

Conclusions

In this chapter I have tried to demonstrate that there is no hard and fast distinction between free intellectual speech and commercial speech and that there should be no automatic assumption that different rules must apply to both. I have pointed out that the scope of advertising regulation has expanded enormously since its beginnings sixty years ago. From a concern with the often justified complaints of the general public against misleading advertisements and sharp practices of a minority of advertisers, it is now part of a wider paternalistic and neo-puritan project to shape the behaviour of the general population – ironically, it is the regulators who are today's 'hidden persuaders'.

Although it is a defensible classical liberal view that there should be no regulation of commercial speech beyond that of other forms of utterance, there was probably not much wrong with the original brief that advertising should be 'legal, decent, honest and truthful'. The newer concepts of 'harm' and 'offence' are far too widely drawn. They increasingly inhibit the creative freedom of the UK advertising industry, for a long time among world leaders in the field, and they increase uncertainty for businesses which wish to play by the rules but also need to reach consumers as they are, not as regulators and vociferous advocacy groups wish them to be. The ambitions of regulators for further expansion of their powers threatens wider freedoms of expression and attempts to impose a single view of how we should see the world.

Restrictions on what businesses can say in an advertisement have increased, are increasing and ought to be diminished.

8 ATTACKS ON FREEDOM TO SPEAK AND TO PRAY

Philip Booth

Introduction

Freedom of speech is generally regarded as a fundamental human right and is often protected in constitutions. Such protection is meaningless unless people are allowed to say things which others do not like or, indeed, say things which offend other people.

The restrictions on freedom of speech discussed in this chapter are linked to freedom to pray and to freedom of conscience. However, that link is not intrinsic to the argument. It just happens to be the case that the legal cases presented here involve Christians, but they also relate to issues which divide society more generally. Many activists in the abortion debate, which I cover below, are non-believers who share the views of many Christians in relation to the protection of life in the womb. However, it is important to make the link between freedom of speech and religion because this touches upon questions of freedom of conscience, which is also generally regarded as a fundamental human right.

The Catholic Church outlined its teaching on the matter of religious freedom in *Dignitatis Humanae*, one of the documents of the Second Vatican Council.[1] The full English title of the document was 'Declaration on Religious Freedom, on the Right of the Person and of Communities to Social and Civil Freedom in Matters Religious'. Paragraph 3 of that document is very clear:

> It follows that he is not to be forced to act in a manner contrary to his conscience. Nor, on the other hand, is he to be restrained from acting in accordance with his conscience, especially in matters religious ... No merely human power can either command or prohibit acts of this kind ... Injury therefore is done to the human person and to the very order established by God for human life, if the free exercise of religion is denied in society, provided just public order is observed.

All persons must be able to express verbally and in the written word their religious beliefs individually and in association with others: 'The demand is likewise made that constitutional limits should be set to the powers of government, in order that there may be no encroachment on the rightful freedom of the person and of associations' (*Dignitatis Humanae*, 1).

Of course, there are boundaries to such freedoms. The rights of others should not be infringed as 'society has the

---

1   https://www.vatican.va/archive/hist_councils/ii_vatican_council/docu ments/vat-ii_decl_19651207_dignitatis-humanae_en.html

right to defend itself against possible abuses committed on the pretext of freedom of religion' (*Dignitatis Humanae,* 7).

This principle of freedom of speech and conscience, as well as its limits, has generally been widely accepted in secular societies. Deliberately encouraging the use of violence or promoting racial hatred, for example, are categories of abuse that would be restrained by the law. However, saying things that might offend people has not normally been prohibited by the law.

So, for example, the UK Equality and Human Rights Commission states in relation to the Human Rights Act[2]:

> Article 9 protects your right to freedom of thought, belief and religion ... You also have the right to put your thoughts and beliefs into action. This could include your right to wear religious clothing, the right to talk about your beliefs or take part in religious worship.

It continues: 'Public authorities cannot interfere with your right to hold or change your beliefs, but there are some situations in which public authorities can interfere with your right to manifest or show your thoughts, belief and religion.'

This chapter provides examples which show that freedom of speech and conscience in the UK have been restricted in ways that go far beyond what has generally been deemed acceptable in a free society. Much of the chapter

---

2   Article 9: Freedom of thought, belief and religion (https://www.equality humanrights.com/en/human-rights-act/article-9-freedom-thought-be lief-and-religion).

uses the example of protests or vigils in relation to abortion. In doing so, it allows some consistency of argument in relation to the key points. Other issues are covered in the later parts of the chapter.

Restrictions on freedom of speech, conscience, prayer and thought

Public Space Protection Orders

The first case we will examine relates to a direct prohibition on freedom of speech and, indeed, freedom to pray. Given that atheists would define prayers to include 'silent reflection', this prohibition, in effect, bans silent reflection in a public place.

Under the Anti-social Behaviour, Crime and Policing Act 2014, local authorities can prohibit activities within a specific space if the local authority believes that the activity is detrimental to the quality of life of the local community. The order can be renewed an indefinite number of times. The local authority only needs to have 'reasonable grounds' for its action.

A Public Space Protection order (PSPO) has been used by the London Boroughs of Ealing and Richmond to prohibit prayer and speech in a public space. Several others are under consideration. Specifically, after some years of peaceful prayer vigils outside an abortion centre in Ealing, a series of demonstrations was launched against those holding the prayer vigils by an organisation called 'Sister Supporter'. The group organising the counter demonstration then raised a petition to have the vigils banned. Following this, the council then issued a PSPO prohibiting 'protesting, namely engaging in any act of approval/disapproval or attempted act of approval/disapproval, with respect to issues related to abortion services, by any means. This includes but is not limited to graphic, verbal or written means, prayer or counselling....'.

This order explicitly prevents individuals from praying, even silently, or speaking to individuals about alternatives to abortion or offering support as they approach the clinic. It also prohibits the expression of opinions. The High Court and Court of Appeal upheld the Ealing PSPO on the ground that those who wished to be outside the clinic undertaking the prohibited activities 'had a detrimental effect on the quality of life of those visiting the centre which was, or was likely to be, of a persistent or continuing nature' (*Dulgerhiu v. London Borough of Ealing*).

Interestingly, Dulgerhiu herself took the case because she believed that she would have aborted her own baby had it not been for a vigil outside the clinic which she visited. An individual who was part of the vigil provided a leaflet offering practical assistance to Dulgerhiu when her baby was born – help which was subsequently necessary. The vigil therefore widened her options and addressed one of the concerns that often lead pregnant women to seek abortions.

Other attempts have been made outside the PSPO framework to prevent people praying or standing with placards outside abortion clinics. For example, Nottingham City Council took out an injunction against John

Edwards, who was part of a small group praying outside a hospital in Nottingham. This was overturned by the judge, who stated that the council's action could 'simply not be justified'. The nature of the actions outside the clinic is perhaps indicated by the statement from one woman who said that she heard: 'some chanting, possibly in Latin, which she found to be intimidating and sinister'. All published pictures of the vigils suggest small numbers of people (four or fewer), praying silently with small placards with slogans such as 'pray to end abortion'.[3]

When can freedom of speech be restricted? The buffer zone campaign

There have been threats to extend this prohibition on silent prayer and free speech around abortion clinics further. The Home Office launched an inquiry in November 2017 to review legislation surrounding protests and other activities close to abortion centres. Essentially, the proposal on the table was for buffer zones similar to the Ealing PSPO to be created around all clinics enforced by national legislation. The then Secretary of State for the Home Office, Sajid Javid, reported back to parliament in September 2018[4] rejecting that proposal. In his statement he noted that only around

---

3 See, for example, Anti-abortion group 40 Days for Life targets Queen's Medical Centre. BBC News, 14 February 2018 (https://www.bbc.co.uk/news/uk-england-nottinghamshire-43006171). A counter-demonstration is also pictured with ten people taking part.

4 Outcome of the Abortion Clinic Protest Review, 13 September 2018 (https://www.parliament.uk/business/publications/written-questions-answers-statements/written-statement/Commons/2018-09-13/HCWS958).

10 per cent of abortion clinics experienced a protest of any kind and that few of these protests were in any sense aggressive. Most involved passive activities.

The Secretary of State also noted that there was existing legislation available to deal with problems that any protests may cause:

> In making my decision, I am also aware that legislation already exists to restrict protest activities that cause harm to others. For example, under the Public Order Act 1986, it is an offence to display images or words that may cause harassment, alarm or distress. This Act also gives the police powers to impose conditions on a static demonstration if they believe it may result in serious public disorder, serious damage to property or serious disruption to the life of the community or if the purpose of the assembly is to intimidate others. There are also offences under the Protection from Harassment Act 1997 when someone pursues a course of conduct which they know will amount to the harassment of another person.

This takes us directly to the question of where the state should restrain freedom of speech.

One principle by which we might judge whether action to prevent freedom of speech is justified is J. S. Mill's 'harm principle'. According to this principle, government intervention is regarded as justified only if the speech harms others. This is a principle that is often used as a guide to policy by those who would describe themselves as social liberals. In framing his harm principle, however, Mill specifically included inciting violence as a reason for restricting freedom of speech, but he specifically excluded hurting the feelings of others as a reason for restriction (Mill 2006, chapters 3 and 2 respectively). The activities that are prevented by the PSPO – prayer, handing out counselling leaflets or holding up posters – neither incite violence nor cause physical harm. As noted above, whether they hurt the feelings of others or help others psychologically is also debatable.

Prohibiting prayer and free speech on the grounds that it causes psychological harm, widely defined, is not a tenable argument for a stable legal framework in a free society. While it can be argued that an individual praying outside an abortion clinic causes psychological harm to those entering, it can also be argued that the act of entering the clinic and continuing with an abortion can cause psychological harm to those who oppose the procedure. Both are legal activities of which others disapprove. PSPOs are inhibiting freedom of speech in public places even where there is no question of incitement to violence. In fact, the Acts of Parliament to which Sajid Javid referred and the relevant case law are already somewhat more restrictive than is implied as appropriate by Mill.

One particular example is of interest in setting the parameters of that Act. In a case involving Andy Stephenson and Kathryn Sloane, who were arrested under the Act in Brighton in 2010 for holding images depicting abortion outside a clinic, the judge outlined the meaning of harassment, alarm and distress in law.

Those holding such signs liken what they do to the actions of anti-slave-trade protesters in the nineteenth century and argue that, by holding images, they are simply presenting facts which they would like others to view so that they reconsider their views. The judge reasoned that a complainant's feelings of 'distress' or 'alarm' under Section 5(b) of the Public Order Act are only actionable if they are caused by a sign which is objectively 'abusive' or 'insulting' and that this requires the signs to be demeaning or disparaging to foreseeable viewers. Because the pictures in this case were medically accurate, they can, it was argued, neither demean nor disparage: they do not involve the expression of an opinion but illustrate what happens in the abortion process.[5]

It is interesting that those who support buffer zones and further restrictions on free speech often begin by suggesting that they respect the right to free speech, but then argue that it is a qualified right and use as their cited qualification the language that appears in the Public Order Act. For example, the Mayor of London, Sadiq Khan, has said: 'The right to peaceful protest must be respected, but we must never tolerate behaviour that seeks to deliberately harass and intimidate women'; and Raj Chada, criminal defence lawyer and protest specialist at London law firm Hodge Jones & Allen, argues that the arguments against PSPO-enforced buffer zones are

---

5 A contrast could be made here with the holding of a placard reading 'Women who have abortions are murderers', which may be somebody's opinion that some may think appropriate to express in certain situations. However, to wave such a placard outside an abortion clinic, especially given the law and its definition of both abortion and murder, would be abusive and designed to cause distress.

'erroneous' because '[t]he right to free speech is a qualified right, but when your actions harass or intimidate others, then your right to free speech can be curtailed'.[6] This is a particularly strange argument from a lawyer because the kind of actions cited by Khan and Chada are already illegal under the Public Order Act and the Protection from Harassment Act and case law has already established the meaning of these words: its meaning does not cover the kind of actions that Khan and Chada wish to prohibit using PSPOs.

It would seem that, under the interpretation of the legislation by the courts, the law as it stands both protects free speech and allows women to take all lawful actions to end their pregnancies without being impeded. On the other hand, PSPOs are being used to undermine the freedom to protest, speak, stand and hold placards, give out leaflets or even pray silently. As well as the risk of proliferation of PSPOs, there are other instruments that can be used against individuals that have a similar effect.

Community Protection Notices: the Waltham Forest case

Community Protection Notices (CPNs) apply to individuals rather than to a geographical area. They can be issued by an officer of a local authority to individuals in order

---

6 Stalking, 'lies' and harassment: the fight to enforce buffer zones outside abortion clinics. *The Independent*, 7 November 2019 (https://www.inde pendent.co.uk/life-style/women/abortion-clinic-buffer-zones-uk-home -office-review-bpas-marie-stopes-london-a9188041.html).

to restrict their behaviour. They are very similar in legal standing to a PSPO.

One local authority, the London Borough of Waltham Forest, has used a CPN to restrict freedom of speech in relation to a protest against abortion. In this case, the individual concerned was simply protesting about the law which he wanted to change: it was not a vigil outside an abortion clinic.

The case involved a member of the Centre for Bio-ethical Reform UK, Christian Hacking, who was protesting about abortion. He used large images of an aborted foetus to draw attention to the local Member of Parliament's view on decriminalisation of abortion including of viable babies. A CPN was issued and the person on whom it was served appealed that it was a contravention of his right to free speech. It was argued by a supporter of the appellant that this image was similar to displaying images of tissue or organs damaged by cancer. This might be done in public health campaigns to influence attitudes towards smoking, for example.

The CPN notice and the basis for turning down the appeal was that the image had a persistent negative effect on the quality of lives of the community.[7] In his evidence the appellant produced credible examples of where images had changed public opinion in the past, arguing that the

---

7   The full judgement can be found at https://christianconcern.com/wp-con tent/uploads/2018/10/CC-Resource-Judgment-Hacking-LBWF-200506 .pdf?utm_source=Christian+Concern&utm_campaign=f2d4c74480 -BN-202000506-Hacking-Walthamstow&utm_medium=email&utm_term =0_9e164371ca-f2d4c74480-127561849).

images he was using were attempting to change public opinion in the same way. It was further argued that the question of abortion involved two strongly opposed sides and that the CPN allowed one side to veto the message of the other side.

The judge found that the display of the images had a detrimental effect on some people in the locality. The judge also concluded that the effect was continuing in the case of two witnesses and that their health was affected. In addition, the judge found that there was, in the area of the display, behaviour which was 'feisty' as well as some disorder.

In the judgement, Article 10 of the Convention on Human Rights was quoted:

> The exercise of these freedoms [political speech], since it carries with it duties and responsibilities, may be subject to such formalities, conditions, restrictions or penalties as are prescribed by law and are necessary in a democratic society, in the interests of national security, territorial integrity or public safety, for the prevention of disorder or crime, for the protection of health or morals, for the protection of the reputation or rights of others, for preventing the disclosure of information received in confidence, or for maintaining the authority and impartiality of the judiciary.

The judge found that the appellant was served with the CPN in the pursuit of the legitimate aims of maintaining order and protecting health.

This reasoning and judgement is problematic. It effectively means that those who oppose a particular political viewpoint can have the expression of that viewpoint prohibited by a council officer who uses a civil device. This can happen if opponents create the circumstances in which there will be a breach of the peace or if a tiny number of people are distressed by the image. This is not only a restriction on freedom of speech, it is achieved by a device wielded by a council officer which can be activated according to entirely arbitrary criteria.

It might be argued that councils should be able to determine what type of protests take place on or near their own property or on public highways. Organisations cannot have carte blanche to undertake any activities they like on any piece of public land. But such restrictions should be general and not arbitrary. For example, it could be argued that large stationary gatherings or large placards that cause an obstruction should be prohibited by council by-laws. However, these should be general prohibitions passed by the council. The problem with CPNs is the same as the problem with PSPOs. Both allow council officers who might be motivated by personal preference or their own political views or the political views of a small interest group to prohibit free speech, or even to prohibit praying, using a much lower bar than is intended by the law that parliament has passed in relation to free speech.

We know where you live: free speech and police visits

There has also been concern about restrictions on freedom of speech arising from the hate crime provisions built into the Equality Act 2010. In general, the problems seem to come, not from prosecution under the Act, but from police investigations which can easily be triggered. Two cases illustrate the problem.

In the first, a Baptist Church in Norfolk displayed a poster suggesting that, if you did not believe in God, you would go to hell. The bottom of the poster depicted flames.[8] This is standard Christian teaching for some (though not for all) Christian denominations. Nevertheless, a 20-year-old complained to the police stating that he believed that Christianity is inclusive and loving in nature. A Christian would, of course, regard it as both inclusive and loving behaviour to spread the gospel. The police registered the poster as a 'hate incident'. The police stated: 'National guidance required us to investigate the circumstances and the matter has been recorded as a hate incident. Having spoken to the pastor of the church, it has been agreed the poster will be taken down.'[9] There seems to be no doubt that the police believed that they were required to register the poster as a hate incident, that they visited the pastor and that the visit caused the poster to be removed.

In the second case, Oluwole Ilesanmi was arrested and questioned by the Metropolitan Police for alleged hate

8   Amusingly, the poster was next to another poster promising visitors to the church a very warm welcome.

9   Police investigate Attleborough church 'hate incident' after sign suggests non-Christians will 'burn in hell' – but what do you think? *Eastern Daily Press*, 22 May 2014 (https://www.edp24.co.uk/news/police-investigate-at tleborough-church-hate-incident-after-sign-suggests-non-christians-will -burn-in-hell-but-what-do-you-think-1-3612263).

speech crimes. He was then released and awarded £2,500 compensation for wrongful arrest and humiliating and distressing treatment.

In addition to the direct impact of police involvement on free speech in both cases, there will be an indirect effect. Few people wish to go through a police investigation and may be put off from speaking freely because they are worried about the consequences.

According to the principles outlined by Mill and also those enshrined in UK law, it should be unacceptable for the law to prevent any individual or religious group talking publicly about 'eternal damnation' except in very limited circumstances such as when the term is used as a deliberate part of a process of mental intimidation of an individual. There will always be cases, of course, where the police interview or even arrest people in circumstances that turn out to be inappropriate. However, in this case, arguably, the law encourages such action.

A hate crime is defined by the Crown Prosecution Service (CPS) in the following way:

> The term 'hate crime' can be used to describe a range of criminal behaviour where the perpetrator is motivated by hostility or demonstrates hostility towards the victim's disability, race, religion, sexual orientation or transgender identity ... A hate crime can include verbal abuse, intimidation, threats, harassment, assault and bullying, as well as damage to property.[10]

---

10 https://www.cps.gov.uk/hate-crime

The CPS advice also sets a high hurdle for a successful prosecution. The problem is that incidents are recorded as hate incidents by the police, and have to be investigated as such, if, in the opinion of the alleged victim or any other person, an incident was motivated by hatred or prejudice based on one of the stated characteristics in the Equality Act. This can lead to controversial but reasonable opinions being the basis of a visit from the police or even arrest. It is easy to see how the threat of the reporting of a hate incident may stifle free speech and debate. Indeed, in both cases above, such action led to the cessation of the activity. Many people will simply not wish to encounter the police in the course of their daily lives and they should not feel inhibited from speaking freely for fear that they might do so.

A close-run thing: *Lee v. McArthur and Ashers*

A further case of a rather different type relates to a cake shop in Northern Ireland managed by a Christian couple. The couple was asked to bake a cake for a gay person. The couple did not actually know the prospective purchaser was gay and this has not been disputed. The bakers were asked to put the slogan 'Support Gay Marriage' on the cake. After discussion within the family firm, the customer was told that the order could not be fulfilled because the bakery was a Christian business and they did not wish to promote gay marriage. This case is especially interesting because it provides one of the few modern examples in a free country of persons being required to say something they did not believe rather than being prevented from saying something they did believe, which is the topic of the earlier discussion.

In the judgements in the lower courts, it was held that the action of the bakers was direct discrimination because it was the insertion of the word 'gay' before 'marriage' into the slogan that led to the order not being accepted. The judge therefore determined that this was discrimination even though the suppliers did not know the purchaser was gay and even though they would have supplied a cake for a gay wedding but without that slogan (or, for that matter, would not have supplied a cake for a heterosexual wedding with a slogan on it which supported gay marriage: a scenario that is not entirely implausible).

This interpretation is especially interesting because, if the judgement of the lower courts had been upheld, it would then be the case that anti-discrimination law was not only requiring a business to provide a service to somebody living in a way that the business owners regarded as sinful, but would have required them to write a slogan promoting a particular way of life and promoting a political position of which they did not approve. Also interesting in this case is the fact that the perceived problem in this case is not discrimination against a person as such.

The decision was overturned on appeal to the Supreme Court, which made the distinction between refusing to serve a gay person and refusing to make a statement that went against the business owners' beliefs. It was stated in the judgement that 'nobody should be forced to have or express a political opinion in which he does not believe'; that 'the bakery would have refused to supply this particular cake to anyone ... there was no discrimination on grounds of sexual orientation'; and that 'no justification has been shown for the compelled speech which would be entailed'.[11]

This case is worth noting because of how far it could have limited freedom of conscience. If the original judgements had stood, people could have been required to express support for a political idea that they oppose.

Free speech and institutional culture

There are many other examples of actions which lead to suggestions that free speech is under threat in society. In particular, free speech on campuses is regularly in news headlines and is a subject taken seriously by the government. Universities UK (2014) provides a detailed discussion of the legal and other considerations for universities in relation to promoting free speech. Universities do have a legal obligation to protect free speech and academic freedom under the Education Act 1986 and related legislation. However, this is subject to a range of other obligations.

Nevertheless, there has been considerable concern about a large number of specific events or decisions that are regarded by many as undermining free speech or, at least, creating a climate of intolerance. One such example is the cancelling of a Visiting Fellowship in the Faculty of Divinity at the University of Cambridge for the academic

---

11 *Lee* (Respondent) *v Ashers Baking Company Ltd and others* (Appellants) (Northern Ireland). The judgement can be found at https://www.sup remecourt.uk/cases/docs/uksc-2017-0020-judgment.pdf.

Jordan Peterson after protests from students and staff. Commenting on the decision, a staff spokesperson said: '[Cambridge] is an inclusive environment and we expect all our staff and visitors to uphold our principles. There is no place here for anyone who cannot [do so].' The Student Union commented: 'His work and views are not representative of the student body and as such we do not see his visit as a valuable contribution to the University, but one that works in opposition to the principles of the University.'[12]

This last comment is especially interesting as it suggests quite directly that Cambridge University Student Union believes that people whose views are not representative of those of the student body cannot make a valuable contribution to the university. This seems to undermine the whole essence not just of freedom of expression but also academic freedom and academic inquiry. The university's behaviour, prima facie, does not seem to be consistent with the Vice-Chancellor's expressed aspiration that: 'Cambridge is the natural home for all those who want to challenge ideas, and are prepared to have their ideas challenged.'[13]

There are many other examples of guest speakers being 'no platformed' in universities even if they are part of the political mainstream or because they hold feminist views questioning certain theories on transsexuality.

---

12 The quotations from the student union and from Cambridge University are to be found in Cambridge University rescinds Jordan Peterson invitation. *The Guardian*, 20 May 2019 (https://www.theguardian.com/educa tion/2019/mar/20/cambridge-university-rescinds-jordan-peterson-invita tion).

13 Vice-Chancellor's address to the university, October 2019.

In a different context, a Christian doctor was dismissed by the Department for Work and Pensions (DWP) after using sex-at-birth rather than preferred gender pronouns when undertaking health assessments for people claiming benefits. The judgement in relation to the case determined that, while the doctor had a right to hold those beliefs under the Equality Act 2010, the right to manifest them was subject to the right of the client to be called by their preferred pronoun under the provisions of the same act. Not to use the preferred pronoun of the client would be discrimination and harassment under the Act.[14]

A Christian doctor, Dr Richard Scott, was also investigated by the General Medical Council (GMC) in 2012 for talking about his faith to a patient. Unusually, the GMC allowed the complainant to give evidence by telephone without any cross-examination. The complaint was upheld and the doctor given a warning. The GMC has undertaken a further 'fitness to practice' investigation into the same individual after receiving complaints not from any patients but from the National Secular Society about the individual talking to patients about his faith. However, that was not taken further.

Interestingly, Dr Scott's practice clearly states on the opening page of its information booklet that the majority of its partners are Christians and that their faith guides how they view their responsibilities towards their patients. They state that they will offer to talk to patients about

---

14   *Mackereth v The Department for Work and Pensions and others.* The judgement seems to reflect a priority ranking of protected rights.

spiritual matters but that patients are free to reject this offer or to make clear that they would not like the offer to be made.[15]

These examples all have different implications for freedom of speech and the approach we might wish to take in a free society would be different in each case. In the case of universities, they are free and independent institutions. In a free society, however reprehensible we might regard the behaviour of a particular institution, universities should surely be free to decide their own policies with regard to freedom of speech, as long as they fulfil their charitable objectives. If central government were to impose a blueprint in relation to how free speech should be ensured within universities, it would risk undermining the plurality of the sector.[16]

As far as the provision of medical services is concerned, in principle, in a free society, we should surely welcome a plurality of institutions based on different values and approaches to providing medical care. Such freedom exists in many other countries where medical service providers often have religious foundations. It also exists in the hospice and social care sectors in the UK. The problem appears to be that the GMC has a statutory role in licensing doctors. And, as a state licensing body, it is restricting how doctors can deliver medicine alongside other forms of patient support even if the practice is made clear to patients.

---

15 https://www.practicebooklet.co.uk/bethesda/online/

16 For example, the London School of Economics was founded to promote the objectives of the socialist Fabian society and there are many universities with a Christian foundation in a pluralist higher education sector.

Newman's 'Idea of a University' discussed the importance of not detaching medicine from philosophy and religion (Newman 1852). People are free to disagree with this perspective, but surely it should be possible to tie one's faith overtly to the practice of medicine.

These cases raise a further set of issues, discussed by Oderberg (2018), related to whether individuals should have freedom of speech and conscience protected in sectors where there are monopoly or monopsony characteristics. But, in general, in a free society we should not need to legislate to protect freedom of speech and conscience. We should simply avoid legislation that restricts such freedoms, but there is, nevertheless, a problem when a professional body with an effective statutory monopoly is determining how its members should practise when it comes to their faith.

Conclusion

The use of Public Space Protection Orders and Community Protection Notices leads to clear and significant restrictions on freedom of speech, conscience and prayer which are not compatible with a free society. Such instruments can be employed using administrative discretion without recourse to the courts. On the other hand, the Public Order Act and Protection from Harassment Act, which have been properly tested in the courts, only restrict speech if it is abusive or insulting, demeaning or disparaging. A relatively high bar has been set by the courts for limiting free speech on these grounds. Though some might believe these acts to be insufficiently liberal, as compared with J. S. Mill's perspective on free speech, the limits these laws put on free speech are not onerous.

There are other areas of concern when it comes to freedom of speech and conscience. For example, police will investigate hate incidents if, in the opinion of the alleged victim or any other person, an incident was motivated by hatred or prejudice based on one of the stated characteristics which include religion. As we have seen, police intervention has stopped people speaking freely and fear of a police visit is likely to lead people to self-censor.

The author would not regard J. S. Mill as his philosophical guide. However, the 'harm principle' is often cited by social liberals to justify non-intervention by the state in moral matters. Mill supported freedom of speech and believed that we do not have the right to be protected from speech that offends us unless there is incitement to violence. Our parliamentary legislation broadly respects that principle. However, a range of other legislative devices have given power to government officials or the police to undermine freedom of speech and conscience in a decisive way. These powers are being used and they have no place in a free society.

9 THE THREAT TO FREEDOM OF SPEECH IN UNIVERSITIES IS A SYMPTOM OF A WIDER PROBLEM

Stephen Davies

There are forceful claims that freedom of speech is under threat, not least in higher education, once thought of as being the great fortress of free expression. But there are rejoinders to the effect that these concerns are overstated, or are merely the whining of current losers of debates. Much of the pessimism is overdone but there are grounds for concern – including ones that get little attention.

As ever, historical perspective aids in understanding both where we are now and how it compares with the past. The brutal reality is that for most of recorded history the idea of open discussion and free speech was a heresy. In most historic states and eras, the public doctrine and the general attitude have been that it is a bad idea to allow people to believe whatever they like and an even worse one to have them express the ideas that they have. This was qualified though in several ways, one of which was that certain privileged people were allowed greater licence and there were special places where free enquiry was actually encouraged – but still within limits. The idea of a location where the bounds of speech are wider is important for contemporary debate because of the idea that the university in particular is such a place, or at least should be.

What is true nowadays, however, is that in most developed countries the position that there should be freedom of thought and expression is the orthodoxy. For some time, robust defences of the need to control thought and expression and the benefits of doing so have not been made. Few people now would mount a full-throated defence of the Index of Forbidden Books, for example.[1] Instead we get arguments that are frequently disingenuous, to the effect that while freedom of thought and speech is desirable in the abstract it should not apply in certain cases or under certain circumstances.

Freedom of thought

The reason for this shift in the official pieties about freedom of thought is a complex story. The main element, both a cause and an effect of the shift, was the sustained innovation of all kinds that is the central feature of the modern world. Freedom of thought and speech of a certain degree was essential for this to get started and then sustain itself. This meant among other kinds of change, technological innovations that made effective freedom of thought and expression easier (for example, the powered and rotary printing press). So, there was a self-reinforcing cycle. Many powerful people have tried to allow free discussions of

---

1   For someone who does, see Vermeule (2017).

science and technology (because of the benefits in terms of economic growth and military power) while restraining the conversation in other areas (for fear of the social and political consequences). But experience so far suggests that this is not sustainable.

Alongside what we may call the spontaneous change in attitudes and practices towards speech brought about by technological innovations, there was also sustained political and intellectual campaigning. This took the form of campaigns against official censorship and controls and also against entrenched social attitudes and practices. It is easy to forget how hard fought these were and how recent many of the victories were. In many places this long-term change went along with a decline in the social and political importance of organised religion, given the importance of that as a source of both tacit and explicit barriers to free thought and speech. What the campaigns over specific questions did was to lead to the articulation of generalised arguments in favour of those freedoms, which remain familiar. The arguments in turn were the basis for further objections to controls or limits and so once again a positive feedback loop was created. Finally, alongside the now elaborated arguments was the emergence of institutions that embodied and realised freedom of thought such as the press, publishing, the book trade, the other media (particularly radio and television and, more recently, social media) and (perhaps) educational institutions, above all, universities. This also included the appearance of other places and institutions that facilitated discussion even though that was not their primary purpose, from pubs and social clubs, to hairdressers and beauty salons (Oldenburg 1989).

Limitations on speech

This, however, is still subject to limitations, which come from the very institutions that in other ways make free speech possible. The first of these is property. One of the rights making up the bundle called 'property' is that of being able to regulate or prohibit certain kinds of speech and expression. To take an everyday example, any person has the perfectly legitimate power to prohibit certain kinds of speech or expression in the house that they own. This can be extended to corporate persons or property-owning institutions such as companies or universities. Ayn Rand made this point in her discussion of the Free Speech Movement at the University of California, Berkeley in the 1960s, arguing that there was no right to free speech on somebody else's property – in this case that of the university (Rand 1971: 47). This argument had added force in her case since she was a strong proponent of a Lockean notion of natural rights.

Similarly, a company or employer has a perfect right to regulate or ban certain kinds of expression on company property. As Rand pointed out, this does raise problems where public space and property are concerned but in predominantly market-based societies this is not a general problem.

The second is the role of institutions or corporate bodies, and the powers that they have over members or employees as part of their function. In the case of companies as employers this is straightforward. When someone enters into a contract of employment, the contract may include stipulations as to what the employee may say or express in the way of ideas and opinions, in their capacity as employees or while on company property or business. In this case a distinction is made between this area, which is regulated, and what the employee does in their private capacity outside their employment, which should be their business rather than the employer's. In many cases though there is a prohibition against 'bringing the employer into disrepute' and this is trickier because of the difficulty of defining what this means and the possible result of the employees surrendering the ability to express themselves as they wish *anywhere*. Quite apart from the wider impact on open discourse should this become widespread, there is the separate point that this is an unwarranted extension of private power over individuals into areas that are appropriate only for governments – if even then.[2] In recent times there have been increasing numbers of examples of corporations and other employers trying to control their employees' speech (in the shape of spoken words, tweets and emails) in this way.

The historical basis of university freedoms

However, the major institutions relevant for contemporary discussions of free expression are educational ones, above

---

2 This point is made extensively in Anderson (2019).

all, universities. Most of the angst and alarm focusses on them, although it is starting to shift to concerns about public debate and conversation in general. The focus is on arguments that universities are or should be the central institutions for free enquiry, speech and discussion and that these functions are being systematically undermined. When combined with wider social developments, it is feared that this will restrict conversation and debate of all kinds, intellectual and political. This is because higher education is thought to be critical in maintaining a dynamic balance in society between free discussion, and the social rules that both enable it and constrain it. Universities are held to be special places, where there is greater latitude for expression and argument than in society at large. They are places where intellectual innovation and debate of all kinds can happen before it then spreads out into wider society.

Is this accurate, though? The answer from history is that historically it was not but it did indeed gradually become so in the last hundred and fifty years. Universities are, in their origins, self-governing communities of scholars with a corporate identity that is recognised in law (Rashdall 2010). They are found in several of the world's great civilisations in slightly different forms (see, for example, Lee 2000). The mission is everywhere the same – to pursue scholarship and thereby to increase knowledge and understanding. In the twentieth century, understanding this means that scholars, university faculty and students should be free to express themselves in almost any way and to explore and develop and debate all sorts of ideas, including ones that are regarded by the wider society as subversive or blasphemous. The only limits should be the respect given to fellow intellectuals so that they have an equal right to speak, and the universal limits against speech that deliberately incites criminal acts or provokes immediate danger. Universities are therefore places with a special function, to push debate and discussion to its limits in every field of study and thought. In their corporate capacity they are self-governing and self-regulating, while the position and income of members is unusually secure with dismissal allowed only for a very limited range of egregious breaches of professional standards. This is meant to protect individual dissenting scholars from sanction by university administrators or their colleagues.

This is the theory, and in many parts of the world has been the reality since the end of the nineteenth century. It was not the norm historically. The dominant historical view of the university's function was indeed that of discussing and exploring ideas and arguments so as to come closer to the truth – or at least properly to identify the uncertainty. But the underlying presumption was that there was a definite 'Truth' that was known in outline at least. The job of scholars was to work to refine that 'Truth' and fill in the details. This body of 'True Knowledge' was identified with the claims of revealed religion (particularly in the Christian and Islamic civilisations) or with an authoritative tradition (as in the intellectual traditions of Hinduism, Buddhism and Confucianism[3]). The first was more restrictive but both ways of thinking imposed strong limits on

---

3   For the Confucian case, see Glomb et al. (2020).

what could be done in an institution of higher learning. Their mission was to explore, refine and strengthen an orthodoxy.

We can see this until as recently as the nineteenth century in the UK, when members of the two ancient universities of Oxford and Cambridge were obliged to sign the Thirty-nine Articles of faith and undertake that all of their teaching and writing would conform to their principles and doctrine. This meant that only those prepared to subscribe to the tenets of orthodox Anglicanism could be members of Oxford or Cambridge colleges. There was a similar requirement to conform to the principles of the Church of Ireland at Trinity College, Dublin and to those of the Kirk at the four ancient Scottish universities. Exactly the same pattern was found at universities in the Catholic parts of Europe both before and after the Reformation, with conformity to the doctrine of the Church by scholars supervised by orders such as the Jesuits and Dominicans (and ultimately the Holy Office).

The university as an arena of protected and unrestrained discussion is actually one of the more recent achievements of the liberal movements for free discussion in general that were referred to earlier. Until as late as the early twentieth century most of the real exploration and discussion of ideas did not happen in institutions of higher learning. It happened instead in the pages of the press, above all, the very varied and intellectually heavyweight periodical press (Shattock 2019). It also took place in the plethora of private discussion and debating societies and in several important social institutions, above all, public houses, clubs or associations. In nineteenth-century Europe, public discussion was more varied and widespread because it took place in a much wider range of institutions in both an informal and formalised way.

In Britain the response of those excluded from participation in the intellectual life of the university, both Catholic and Dissenter, was to create their own institutions. Initially, there were Dissenting Academies and many of these developed into institutions that ultimately were given university status, such as the constituent parts of the University of London. Roman Catholics for their part created their own institutions, such as University College Dublin, founded in 1854. This pattern of setting up institutions to explore dissent was a recurring feature of Chinese history as well.

Challenges to free speech in universities

If we look at the complaints being made (typically by conservatives but increasingly by people from the centre-left as well) about limitations on speech in universities, on both sides of the Atlantic, we can see that they have three main elements.

The first concerns pressure from students to have certain forms of speech either hedged about with warnings or even banned outright (see Haidt and Haslam 2016; Friedersdorf 2016). In some cases, this pressure takes the form of physical protests and attempts to prevent lectures or talks from taking place.

The second is that of pressure or sanctions against academics by university administrators, in response either to pressure from the student body or to a media furore (usually on Twitter) over things said or supposedly said by a member of staff (McCullogh 2020). This is more serious than the first because students do not actually have authority – it is only the administrators who can act and impose sanctions.

The third complaint, particularly common in the US but increasingly heard in the UK and the Commonwealth, is that of ideological uniformity among faculty – they may not have to subscribe formally to a contemporary version of the Thirty-nine Articles but they might as well. This complaint is well founded – there are many surveys of American faculty, for example, that show a remarkable degree of political consensus among them (Maranto et al. 2009; but see also Jaschik 2017).

These three specific complaints are united by a more general observation, which is that, on the evidence of university students, younger people are peculiarly intellectually fragile and unwilling to confront ideas that they find uncomfortable and challenging (Lukianoff and Haidt 2019).

What should we make of this? The first point to make is that the first two elements of complaint are genuine, but overstated. The number of actual incidents is small in proportion to the size of the sector and the number of students. The incidents that happen attract a lot of attention but that is because they are unusual.[4] Moreover, if we look at the

---

4   Threats to free speech at university have been blown out of proportion. *The Times*, 5 December 2019 (https://www.thetimes.co.uk/article/threats -to-free-speech-at-university-have-been-blown-out-of-all-proportion-wg9f 66nmq).

actual events a very clear pattern emerges, which is that they overwhelmingly happen at elite (and in the American case, very expensive) institutions. This is clear in the US, where prominent incidents have happened at top twenty research institutions or leading liberal arts colleges – but hardly ever at state institutions, let alone community colleges. A similar pattern can be seen in the UK, where the major incidents have happened at Cambridge, Oxford, and parts of the University of London. This suggests that many of the ructions about free speech in higher education are not internally generated but arise from something going on outside the university, in wider society.

What about the third, and better founded, concern, over the ideological uniformity of academics? In this connection the points already made about companies also apply to universities, as does the one about property. University administrators who are (in theory at least) acting on behalf of the corporate body of the institution as a whole could perfectly correctly prohibit certain kinds of speech or even specific content of speech if they wish to. In addition, many universities still have a specific corporate mission such as officially Catholic ones where part of the institution's mission is to teach and explore the Faith as defined by the Church. In such cases it is perfectly appropriate for the institution to say that certain kinds of view or argument are incompatible with that mission and cannot be expressed by faculty members if they wish to remain in post. What many in higher education today seem to have is a similar view that the university's role is to promote and explore a particular vision of the truth or at least to systematically exclude certain views and perspectives (heresies in other words). The precise content of this orthodoxy is what is being debated, hence the heat and argument.

This suggests that the problem is not lack of intellectual diversity within the faculty of any one university. The problem is lack of such diversity *between institutions*. If higher education institutions[5] had the range of intellectual diversity that we find in the press or think tanks, the fact of one of them having better than 90 per cent of its faculty with the same kind of political views would not matter anything like as much.

If an orthodoxy has become established, then the thing to do would appear to be that of imitating dissident Confucian scholars or eighteenth- and nineteenth-century Dissenters and setting up separate and independent institutions. Why is this not done? There are two reasons. The first is the overwhelmingly dominant role of government funding in higher education, even in the US. A heterodox institution would have to eschew all of this, to the extent that government is aligned with the dominant orthodoxy, and this is a serious disincentive for both investors and possible faculty. The main reason though is the second one, which is the chief function of higher education in the contemporary world. This is not scholarship, research or debate but the certification of young people so that they have a chance of access to high-paid and high-status roles (Caplan 2018).

---

5   And their means of communication, such as learned journals.

This is why students are prepared to pay large sums of money in tuition and accept the opportunity cost of taking three or four years out of the paid labour force. This central function of modern higher education creates a high barrier to creating new institutions in the manner of nineteenth-century Dissenters and Catholics. The problem is that without official recognition they would not be able to perform the certification function. They would still be able to act as communities of scholars engaged in study, research, teaching and debate but not enough students are currently prepared to pay for that. If an institution cannot play its part in certification, it will not attract enough students or other private finance, as well as not getting government money.

This is part of a wider problem

It is a mistake to focus too narrowly on higher education as the centre of the problem of free discussion and expression. Rather, universities are where a wider problem is manifesting itself most dramatically. What is this wider problem? In very general terms we can identify several major facets to it. The first is the one just identified, the way the combination of government funding (and increasingly also corporate funding) and the meritocratic labour market has corrupted the purpose and nature of the academy, as it became established in the early part of the twentieth century. Another is the impact in this area of the predatory and dysfunctional American legal system. Many of the actions against free expression at present come not from governments but rather from private firms, and institutions such as university administrations. These are driven in many cases by the fear of costly lawsuits brought in the US and this means that any firm that either trades in the US or has business relations with ones that do will be affected by this. In the case of the academy, particularly in Anglophone countries, the problem is the enormous influence of the American higher education system on its counterparts worldwide, particularly at the elite level.

Indeed, we can clearly see that if there is a problem of attempts to constrain speech in liberal democracies (as opposed to authoritarian ones such as China, where this has always been a feature of the regime) it is one with its epicentre in the US. There it is a part of the wider phenomenon of the progressive crisis of the American political and social order, which we can see working out in real time in news bulletins. Much of this is peculiar to the US and grows out of that country's particular history and institutions but other parts are found elsewhere as well. It is just that these phenomena are more pronounced in the US, or, alternatively, they have been exported from there to the rest of the world.

The mud fight

The first thing to note is that we do not have an overwhelmingly powerful movement imposing a set of norms and limits on thought, much as some would like to see it that way. The whole point is that there is enormous controversy and debate, that is why this topic is constantly in the news.

What is actually going on is an argument about where the boundaries for acceptable speech should be, with provocateurs on all sides trying both to push the boundaries out in the direction they favour while looking to push it back on the side they oppose.

There are at least two such groups which want to restrict freedom of expression significantly, for a range of possible reasons. One is a form of populist conservatism, the other, which gets more attention, is a species of radical leftist politics that has intellectual roots in post-modernism and critical theory. Both of these competing factions see themselves as embattled and edgy, in conflict with an establishment, while being portrayed by their opponents as themselves powerful and agenda-setting. The reality is more like a confused mud fight, with intellectual and political tendencies putting a huge amount of effort into trying to define and enforce new limits on what is acceptable and to then narrow them.

It is vanishingly unlikely that any one of them will succeed in doing this in a contemporary developed society. That is because of there being many people and (more importantly) resources opposed to any one position. In addition, new technologies have made it much easier for dissenting views to find expression by reducing the direct cost of expressing views, in the way that the rotary printing press and linotype did over a hundred years ago. If any single intellectual faction seems to be gaining the upper hand, it will provoke organised dissent and the creation of rival institutions (news networks, journals, think tanks, educational institutions) on the part of its opponents. This could be dealt with by resort to censorship and overt force, but few people are so far advocating this. The overwhelmingly likely outcome will be a process of 'pillarisation', with the consolidation of distinct intellectual and cultural subsocieties.[6] This would be better than outright authoritarian censorship but would still be costly in terms of reducing the amount of cultural and intellectual innovation that takes place.

Right now, one of the competing factions is particularly noisy and aggressive and is increasingly provoking a response from others, beyond its mirror image on the populist side. Why though is this faction (the so-called 'woke' or 'social justice' left) in particular making so much noise? This has a sociological explanation. It is because the people who collectively form this movement are from a distinct social formation, members of which are disproportionately found in certain places and institutions, above all the mass media and social media and academia. This is the class of graduate professionals who are the product of a small number of elite institutions (they are themselves a subset of the wider social class of metropolitan graduate professionals). Because people from this class origin occupy a massive preponderance of positions in media, including publishing, and also academia, and play a central role in contemporary politics their concerns and agitations receive disproportionate attention.

So, the mud fight over the location of the limits to speech has two fronts. One is between the graduate

---

6   'Pillarisation': https://en.wikipedia.org/wiki/Pillarisation

professional class in general and the opposition it has provoked in the shape of 'populist' politics. The other is within the professional class, between a majority committed to a kind of generic liberalism or social democracy and a militant minority espousing a collection of positions and beliefs. These include both a form of identity politics that manages to somehow combine radical subjectivism and a form of essentialism, and a radical environmentalism. This is a competition for social status within what is an elite. It is fierce for a simple reason. The source of position within this social formation is by using accreditation from top-ranked institutions to get high-status jobs and roles. The problem is that there is an overproduction of qualified graduates and not enough positions, leading to a competition which increasingly has a generational quality. Why though should this take the form of an argument about what is said at universities?

Intra-class conflict

One reason is that several of the key institutions of the 'new class' are ones centrally involved in the production and dissemination of ideas such as universities, publishing and the media. Limiting what can be said and purging dissenters are ways of winning the struggle to control access to these valuable positions. This increasingly spills over into other important forms of employment for the professional graduate class, such as management in corporate industry and public services, where the tension caused by increasing supply of qualified people and stagnant or declining numbers of positions is also becoming acute. This is a materialist explanation based on people adopting strategies in accordance with economic interests.

The other explanation is ideas-driven and relates to the dominant idea of the contemporary educational world, a central belief for the professional class: the idea of meritocracy. In this frame success is down to merit, defined as talent plus effort and measured by academic attainment. One problem is that the system in practice works in ways that advantage some social groups and disadvantage others, which in terms of the belief itself is seen as illegitimate. Another is that merit in this way of thinking means not just demonstrated ability but moral standing and praiseworthiness. It is this that explains the emphasis on purity of thought that is such a feature of current arguments. One way of showing that you have more merit than someone else who has the same formal qualifications is to show that you have greater virtue and purity or praiseworthiness and are therefore more deserving while they are not (Pluckrose and Lindsay 2020). Arguments about what should or can be said are a way of demonstrating this while trapping the unwary who find they have not kept up with the programme.

This kind of intra-class conflict and political tension plays out in arguments over expression and attempts to limit it. It would be no more than an amusing spectator sport were it not for other features of the contemporary world, which have weakened the social framework for free thinking and expression that developed over the last three hundred years. One is the way that the university and a relatively small number of media outlets have become the dominant location for the more unrestricted exploration of ideas. If we compare the present situation to that of even fifty years ago, it is clear that there has been a dramatic decline in the number of range and places where discussion takes place. Most important is the decline of 'third place' locations that are neither workplace nor the home and which are also not public but not private in a strictly exclusive sense (Oldenburg 1989, 2000; see also Lasch 1995). In theory this has been replaced by the Internet, with chatrooms and message boards providing a replacement for the pubs, beauty parlours and barbershops discussed by Oldenburg. However, there are obvious differences (such as nuance and humour) between the physical face-to-face contact and exchange in third places and their virtual counterparts. It is not clear that the latter can ever be a complete replacement for the former.

Another problem with the idea that the Internet and social media can be a new form of the thick and interconnected ecology of social institutions for discussion and expression that grew up previously, is that while the content is far more diverse and pluralistic than that of the older media, there are only a small number of platforms or providers. There is only one Twitter or YouTube, no matter how many people tweet or post. This has two obvious risks, that the platforms will be regulated by the state on some pretext, or that the platforms themselves will act to restrict speech and expression. It is the second that has increasingly happened but demands for the first are growing.

It is that decline in pluralism and range that is the real threat to free and open thinking and discussion. The transformation of the university's purpose and its involvement in the intra-class manoeuvring that is going on and in which competitive virtue-signalling plays such a part is an element of this, but this would not be such a difficulty if there was more pluralism as far as institutions for discussion and expression of ideas was concerned. This situation has a number of causes, as we would expect for a complex phenomenon. One is technology and in particular the impact of the specific technology of television. Another is the role of government and the way in which government funding and subsidy has crowded out more varied but less lucrative private provision. This is most obvious in higher education but we can see it elsewhere, even, for example, in stand-up comedy. Nor should we simply blame government here – the role of sponsorship and subsidy by large private firms has also played a large part. All of this is exacerbated but not caused by the dysfunctional politics to which meritocracy increasingly leads.

10 FREE SPEECH: THE FREEDOM THAT TRADE UNIONS FORGOT

Dennis Hayes

Trade unions are no longer trade unions except to an ahistorical nominalist. They were formed by workers to fight for better pay and working conditions. Their strength was based on their ability to make their case to an employer and to protest, demonstrate and, if necessary, hurt the employer by striking until their demands were met. In other words, their strength was based on both free speech and organisation. They had to put their case in words and then work as collective organisations to achieve the demands they articulated. Free speech and organisation were their only weapons in the class war.

Trade unions have abandoned free speech as a principle worth fighting for and, as a direct consequence, they have undermined their own power. The explanation of their rejection of the fight *for*, and their ability to fight *with*, free speech is also the explanation of the collapse of trade unions as organisations. Their demise in terms of membership is well documented but they will continue to be ineffective even if their membership increases. Trade unions cannot revive, however large they may become, because they have taken a self-destructive therapeutic turn.

Disorganised unions

By the end of the last century the trade unions in the UK had been defeated after the major industrial battles of the 1980s. There were no longer seen as organisations to which workers could look to defend their jobs and working conditions. The decline in union membership is evidence of this. The fall was dramatic from the high point of 13.2 million trade union members in 1979 to 6.4 million in 2019 (Department for Business, Energy and Industrial Strategy EBIS 2020a,b). Both employers and unions slowly responded to this situation in parallel ways. Employers began to relate to employees indirectly through human resources departments. This was successful because it was a new ideological approach based on what has been called the 'equal opportunities revolution' (Heartfield 2017). Workers no longer related directly to employers in a way that was part of an economic partnership at work even if the previous relationship was often hostile. The new working relationship was seductively but only seemingly moral. Everyone seemed to be committed to seeking equality of opportunity for all. The defeated and directionless trade unions were won over to this new ideology and, as they embraced it, they changed. 'Equality' objectives began to compete with traditional objectives to improve pay and working conditions. They had some material impact in addressing the former exclusion of women and immigrant workers from the workplace. This is generally seen as a positive change, a move to a fairer and more inclusive focus away from the traditional white, male-dominated workplace. But this shift set the foundations for the therapeutic turn.

The therapeutic turn

The therapeutic turn has its origins not solely in the workplace but in the therapeutic culture in wider society. Therapy culture arose spontaneously in the 1990s and filled a political vacuum at the end of the Cold War. Politicians, policymakers and professionals began to relate to ordinary people in therapeutic ways. They saw them as vulnerable, as potential victims. The new political formation that arose offered therapy to victims (T2V).

T2V became a successful, if unarticulated, way that trade unions could relate to members. Trade union members no longer constituted what Margaret Thatcher labelled 'the enemy within'; they were 'the vulnerable within'. Concerns with stress, bullying, wellbeing and mental health began to move to the centre of trade union campaigns. These concerns resonated and gave trade unions a new way of relating to members that was complementary to the concerns of HR departments. Concerns with 'equal opportunity' in those departments also began to focus on the same themes: stress, bullying, wellbeing and mental health. Both trade unions and HR departments believed that the problems workers faced in the twenty-first-century workplace were essentially psychological and primarily emotional. They saw workers as fragile individuals who needed care and support. A marker of this new turn to helping the 'can't cope' worker is the WorkSmart app launched by the TUC to help individuals cope with their life at work (Trades Union Congress 2018). Although individual trade unions have these therapeutic concerns, it is the TUC, with its 5.5 million members in 48 affiliated organisations, that we can use to illustrate the therapeutic turn. The TUC website has sections on stress, bullying, wellbeing and mental health (Trades Union Congress 2020a–d). These are no longer peripheral concerns but central to the trade union movement. Older concerns with pay and working conditions remain but the case for them is increasingly put in terms of protecting vulnerable workers.

To some it may seem that, despite this new concern with protecting the vulnerable worker, trade unions are still organised but in a way that is more suited to the modern workplace. Of course, they are 'organisations' in a formal sense but not in the older sense that referred to trade unions as organisation that were collectives of individuals with human agency. Trade unions now have a diminished sense of their membership as being made up of individuals who find it hard to cope. The 'can't cope' worker needs therapeutic support from their trade union.

If you 'organise' like this, a trade union will resemble Marx's description of the French peasantry: 'the great mass of the French nation is formed by the simple addition of homonymous magnitudes, much as potatoes in a sack form a sack of potatoes' (Marx 1973: 170). Today's trade unionists are like potatoes connected only by their vulnerability and contained within a trade union sack. As such they lack agency and can achieve nothing. The fault here lies not with workers themselves. If trade unions see their members as vulnerable, their members will also come to see themselves as unable to cope and not as human beings with agency. They will see themselves as victims.

'Organising' a collective of victims in this way is forming a 'union' of sorts but the only case such a 'union' will make to an employer is a plea for help. These pleas will never end as it is now assumed that any emotional distress suffered at work will have long-term consequences and require lengthy therapeutic treatment. We have seen a shift from old-fashioned class war to couch war but this shift to couch war is not conflictual in the way class wars were. Both trade unions and employers want to see workers on the therapy couch (Ecclestone and Hayes 2019).

Trading off free speech for safety

The new therapeutic turn has dire consequences for free speech. Vulnerable trade union members are now seen as needing to be protected from any speech that they may find offensive. Speech that is described as stressful, bullying, emotionally damaging or that threatens their mental health is roundly condemned. Any criticism of individual trade union members is also condemned because trade union members must feel *safe* if they are to cope at work. Criticism, however justified it may or may not be, will make trade union members less able to cope.

It would be a mistake to see this new concern with the emotional state of members as an expression of the weakness of trade unions. Supporting vulnerable workers gives trade unions new authority. They are the protectors of victims and are as invulnerable to criticism as their members. Who would dare criticise a vulnerable, stressed, bullied worker who may be emotionally fragile and have mental health problems? Likewise, who would dare criticise those trade unions who protect vulnerable, stressed, bullied workers who may be emotionally fragile and have mental health problems?

This new authority is powerful. But is not the power of leading a collective of individuals with human agency. Trade unions now see their members as lacking in agency and needing their trade union to protect them. The form of trade unionism may seem familiar, but this is deceptive. Trade unions are now therapeutic organisations and their 'agency' is reduced to pleading.

Free speech and the Prevent duty

It may seem that the continuing opposition of trade unions to the Prevent duty introduced in September 2015 as part of the Counter-Terrorism and Security Act 2015 was an exception to their indifference to free speech. The Act places a legal duty on universities, schools and other bodies to demonstrate that they are countering terrorism and radicalisation. The TUC, and member unions, opposed the Act as an infringement of free speech. But their main thrust was to blame Britain's actions abroad. They also claimed that the duty would create a climate in which Muslim pupils and students would feel insecure and threatened and that this would undermine learning relationships.[1]

At its 2015 congress, the University and College Union (UCU) declared that the Prevent duty 'seriously threatens academic freedom and freedom of speech' (University and College Union 2015). This argument was a bit much coming from the UCU in alliance with the National Union of Students (NUS). Both had supported the 'no platforming' of people they disagreed with for many years (McCormack 2016).

Why 'free speech' was considered an issue for the unions in relation to Prevent was not truly based on their fantasies of a 'right wing' backlash against Muslims and a general rise in 'Islamophobia'. Underneath all the wild political claims was their belief that Muslims were the most vulnerable group in society. They had to be protected.

A speaker at an Institute of Race Relations (IRR) conference in 2015 made this exact criticism of the model that underpins the government's concept of 'radicalisation': 'central to Prevent, is informed by [the] notion of "psychological vulnerability"; that individuals must have *certain vulnerabilities that make them more likely to engage in terrorism*' (Bolloten 2015, author's italics).

But this characterisation of Muslims was not a legislative aberration. It was the mainstream view of institutions and unions (Hayes 2012). In a therapeutic culture British

---

1   TUC 2015: Prevent strategy will destroy teacher and pupil relations. *Morning Star*, 14 September 2015 (https://morningstaronline.co.uk/a-6258-tuc -2015-prevent-strategy-will-destroy-teacher-and-pupil-relations-1).

Muslims, like Palestinians on the international stage, are the ultimate victims. Although the unions' objection to Prevent was sometimes couched in terms of the defence of free speech, it was nothing more than an expression of therapeutic concern. It was not a cynical inconsistency in the unions' general indifference to free speech; it was a statement that these victims were so vulnerable they must not be threatened and were beyond criticism.

Speak up only to whistleblow

Whistleblowing is an important right and is much more than pleading. It has taken on a new importance because of the therapeutic turn. Workers now see themselves as more vulnerable than ever.

Defending the right of whistleblowers to speak out is the one aspect of speech that trade unions cherish. While I was writing this chapter, there were concerns voiced in the media about doctors and other NHS and health-care staff being told not to speak to the press about shortages of equipment.[2] But whistleblowing is about making public wrongdoing at work such as fraud, health and safety breaches, damage to the environment, failing to have insurance, miscarriages of justice or covering up industrial malpractice. It is reporting the bad *behaviour* of companies. In a similar way to putting in complaints or initiating grievance or disciplinary procedures, whistleblowing

---

2   Coronavirus: Doctors 'told not to discuss PPE shortages'. BBC News, 15 May 2020 (https://www.bbc.co.uk/news/uk-52671814).

involves speech but is best considered as behaviour, as an *action*. It involves speech but, as anyone knows who has been involved in any of these internal, formal proceedings, it is not free.

Of course, the desire of any worker to say 'I want to make a complaint, to take out a grievance or invoke a disciplinary procedure, or to whistleblow' is an exercise in free speech. Just as the desire of those who wish to censor, or ban speech is an exercise in free speech against free speech. However, once any of these procedures are initiated, then the 'freedom' to speak is extremely restricted.

Whistleblowing has just one extra freedom. Whistleblowers, unlike those in other workplace proceedings, cannot be subject to non-disclosure agreements, often called 'gagging orders'. The internal workplace process of grievance, discipline and whistleblowing leading to gagging clauses are examples of unfree speech. For example, in many disciplinary procedures going public about your case leads to further disciplinary action. These procedures silence speech to the detriment of workers. It is hard to defend workers in such situations because going public is often the best defence for anyone who is charged with a disciplinary offence. Such charges are increasingly about offensive speech.

The suppression of speech

Putting emphasis on the therapeutic turn in the workplace should not be seen an argument against the fact that unions continue to suppress free speech for political reasons and to ignore the need to defend the free speech of their members (Butcher 2020). These political attacks on free speech continue but they are often rewritten in the therapeutic language of words causing emotional offence and the need for 'safe spaces' for vulnerable groups of workers. The hounding of the so-called TERF (Trans Exclusionary Radical Feminist) academic Selina Todd and others are examples of the new censorship because of emotional offence (Academics for Academic Freedom 2020).

There are still cases of trade unions acting against members for exercising free speech in breach of their 'rules', or, in other words, for thinking independently. Any thoughtful or critical trade unionist is in real danger of being thrown out of a trade union if they dare speak out, even unknowingly, in a way that goes against union policies. Thankfully, most trade unionists are unaware of what left-wing political policies unions adopt at a national level. Their relationship with unions is as individuals. They want protection if they get into difficulties at work. They are not interested in trade union politics.

The most recent high-profile case of someone being thrown out of a union post for speaking out on an issue is that of Paul Embery. Embery was removed from the Fire Brigades Union (FBU) National Executive in 2019 and banned from standing for that role again for two years for speaking in favour of Brexit at a Leave Means Leave rally in contravention of union policy (Riley 2020). Embery paid the price for speaking up for his beliefs after twenty years as a union official. At the time of writing he is challenging the FBU for unfair dismissal. Embery's case is emblematic of the position of trade unionists in relation to free speech. Throughout the Brexit campaign, the trade union movement was largely a remainer movement. Ordinary members kept quiet and showed what they really thought when the 'Red Wall' of northern English constituencies fell to the Tories in order to 'Get Brexit Done!'. There was no free speech about Brexit within trade unions.

No to 'no platform'

Unions also continue to operate policies that 'no platform' right-wing 'extremist' speakers and to ban holders of such views from membership. There is also a section on the TUC website about tackling right-wing extremism (TUC 2020e). This form of censorship is the continuation of a policy adopted by the National Union of Students in the UK in the 1970s (Smith 2020). Whether it is called a 'no platform' policy or not, unions continue supporting the censorious approach that some views must not be heard albeit for new reasons. It is not just political disagreement about racism, fascism, sexism, homophobia or transphobia. The therapeutic shift now requires that any discussion of such ideas – even in universities – is unacceptable as they damage a 'safe and prejudice-free environment' (Smith 2020: 224).

Discussions of 'no platforming' as a policy resemble tedious metaphysical debates as to whether a speaker has been 'no platformed' or just disinvited, or not formally invited to speak, or the meeting itself contravenes a health and safety policy, or there is a threat to public order or to the wellbeing of individuals, or the speaker or members of a panel just pulled out. There are dozens of variations on what are simply attacks on free speech. No platforming is everywhere but it rarely calls itself by its name.

Trade unions can be blunt about 'no platforming' of right-wing extremists as they have policies to exclude right-wing individuals from membership and can happily 'no platform' them or campaign to stop any such speaker from having a 'platform'. They encourage their members to join in their censorship.

Trade unions need to recognise that although banning speakers they disagree with may be permitted by their democratically approved rules, it is an attack on free speech. Firstly, because it is an example of allowing free speech for me but not for you. It is a defence of free speech only for those individuals whose views we approve of. If you believe in free speech you must defend the free speech of those whose views you disagree with. Secondly, this selective approach to free speech reveals a fundamental misunderstanding. Free speech is not just about those speaking but about those who are hearing their speech. If you censor those speaking you are showing contempt for those adults who are hearing that speech. They are implicitly or explicitly being said to be unable to cope with the speech they might hear and may be potentially damaged by it. What was once a simple prohibition of speakers you disagreed with is now a therapeutic protection of vulnerable potential hearers. Trade unions now have a diminished concept of their members that impugns their ability to respond to speech with reason and counter speech.

The therapeutic turn has given the suppression of speech more importance that it previously had. It also makes the suppressors of speech into saintly figures. Trade union officials and members gain untouchable moral authority from their role as protectors of the vulnerable. This new authority is part of the explanation of the shift of many on the political 'left' and the unions towards censorship.

UCU in the therapeutic university

The one trade union above others that should support free speech is the University and College Union. The UCU was formed from the merger of two unions, the Association of University Teachers (AUT) and the National Association of Teachers in Further and Higher Education (NATFHE) in 2006. UCU has over 130,000 members and dominates the further and higher education in the UK and claims to be the largest post-school union in the world. Its record on free speech and academic freedom since its formation has been weak and biased.

An overview of the UCU's approach to free speech illustrates the approaches of many trade unions to free speech. It is not a random choice. Universities are places for intellectual endeavour. Their duty is the pursuit of truth without fear or favour. Universities are also required by law to promote free speech. This has been the case from Section 43 of the Education (No 2) Act 1986 to the recent requirements in the Higher Education and Research Act (2017) that made the new regulator, the Office for Students (OfS) responsible for ensuring that all universities evidence their commitment to free speech or risk a fine or deregistration (Office for Students 2018). It says something of the state of free speech in universities that government finds it necessary to enforce a commitment to free speech.

The UCU represents lecturers and academic-related workers but is behind both the higher education employers and the government in support of free speech and academic freedom. Academic freedom is, of course, more than free speech. It is a continuation and intensification of free speech. Academics are not merely able to express opinions and ideas but are paid to research and develop their ideas and opinions in pursuit of truth. Their freedom is the ultimate expression of freedom of speech.

The therapeutic turn undermines the pursuit of truth in universities. They have become what Kathryn Ecclestone and I labelled 'therapeutic universities'. In the therapeutic university intellectual safety is the over-riding value. From a fringe concern of a few minority groups, the idea that the university must be a 'safe space' for ideas became commonplace. This is a recent development that the online magazine, *Spiked*, drew attention to with its Free Speech University Rankings (FSUR) 2015–2018 (Slater 2019). An inquiry by the parliamentary Joint Committee on Human Rights (JCHR) also found that the misapplication of no platforming and safe space policies were threats to free speech in universities (Weale 2018). The shift in student attitudes to open debate was a direct result of the obsessive concern with 'safeguarding' in schools. Young people now come to university expecting it to be a big school in which they must never feel uncomfortable or emotionally offended and universities encourage this infantilising approach (Ecclestone and Hayes 2019).

How the UCU undermines free speech

The UCU puts free speech and academic freedom far below other values. These values are given in statement 2.5 of its 'Aims and Objects' that commits the trade union and its members:

> To oppose actively all forms of harassment, prejudice and unfair discrimination whether on the grounds of sex, race, ethnic or national origin, religion, colour, class, caring responsibilities, marital status, sexuality, disability, age, migration status, or other status or personal characteristic.

Harassment and discrimination are covered by law. We can put them aside and not elide them with 'prejudice' as this statement does. What counts as 'prejudice' in relation to this long list of 'grounds' is very problematic as is the term 'prejudice' itself (Abrams 2010). This statement means that members will have to curtail and watch their speech and be wary of making any criticism of anyone who falls within one, or more, of this long list of 'grounds' in relation to individuals or groups. It means ensuring that anyone covered by the statement never feels offended and always feels safe. The list is long and in the therapeutic university this policy has come to mean that every student and member of academic staff must always feel emotionally safe. The UCU has further policies that punish members for exercising their freedom of speech to question any of these policies. Rule 6.1 of the trade union makes this clear:

> All members and student members have an obligation to abide by the Rules of the University and College Union, and shall refrain from conduct detrimental to the interests of the Union, from any breach of these Rules, Standing Orders or directions (properly made in accordance with these Rules or Standing Orders) and from all forms of harassment, prejudice and unfair discrimination whether on the grounds of sex, race, ethnic or national origin, religion, colour, class, caring responsibilities, marital status, sexuality, disability, age, or other status or personal characteristic.

There are other rules excluding 'extreme right-wing' but not other extremists from membership:

> UCU will refuse membership to, or expel from existing membership, any person who is a known member or activist of any extreme right-wing political organisation, including the BNP and National Front, where the organisation's aims, objectives and principles are contrary to those of UCU as outlined in 6.1 above.

The policies of the UCU may seem like nothing more than the trade-off of values in the equal opportunities revolution but in the therapeutic university the consequences are disastrous for free speech and academic freedom.

UCU believes in academic freedom BUT ...

The formation of Academics for Academic Freedom (AFAF) in late 2006 led to debates about academic freedom and free speech in the national press. In response to these debates, the UCU conducted a survey of members about academic freedom. What came out of the consultation and discussions in the UCU committees was the Statement on Academic Freedom published in January 2009 (University and College Union 2009). The UCU statement emphasises how academic freedom must be balanced by various duties not to discriminate. It expressed the basic 'but' that equality issues triumph over academic freedom. Or to put it another way, academic freedom only applies to those whose views we support. The UCU does have a track record of supporting some academics who are persecuted for their views but only if they agree with them. The controversial speakers the UCU supports, such as those arguing for an independent Palestine, must be safe to speak. Speakers they disagree with will be denounced because hearing them will make academics and students feel unsafe.

The UCU completely misunderstands academic freedom. It is not merely about an academic's right to teach and discuss their subject without management interference (University and College Union 2012). Academic freedom goes beyond the classroom and requires you to accept freedom of speech throughout the university. It includes the freedom of speech of people who put forward ideas you profoundly disagree with. It does not mean you have to accept their beliefs or opinions. They are subject to the test of criticism. The UCU does not understand the difference between promoting ideas you agree with and academic freedom. They merely wish for the affirmation of acceptable opinion so that everyone can be safe in the therapeutic university.

The UCU Congress 2017 votes for academic freedom

In 2017 the University of Derby branch of the UCU and the East Midlands Regional Committee put a motion to the UCU Congress. The motivation behind the motion was to put academic freedom at the heart of the UCU's activities by making it part of the trade union's aims and objectives. Knowing that it would be opposed if any explicit wording was offered, the formulation of the aim or objective was left to the National Executive Committee. This was a significant move given a recent research report commissioned by the UCU revealed that 87 per cent of members responding wanted more information on what academic freedom meant (University and College Union 2017a). The motion read:

Congress instructs the NEC to bring to Congress in 2018 a statement in defence of academic freedom as an addition to UCU rules Section 2 'Aims and Objects'.

Reflecting on the wording of this amendment, the NEC considered AFAF's principles of academic freedom:

- that academics, both inside and outside the classroom, have unrestricted liberty to question and test received wisdom and to put forward controversial and unpopular opinions, whether or not these are deemed offensive, and
- that academic institutions have no right to curb the exercise of this freedom by members of their staff, or to use it as grounds for disciplinary action or dismissal.

The motion was carried after the bullet points were amended to read:

- that academics and academic-related professional staff should be *free within the law* to question and test received wisdom and to put forward controversial and unpopular opinions, whether or not these are deemed offensive, and
- that employers have no right to curb the free speech of their staff, academic or otherwise, whether on political or commercial grounds, or to penalize them for the honest expression of a point of view. [my italics] (University and College Union 2017b)

The amendment moved by the University of Bath was intended to make the proposal reflect the current legal position in universities. AFAF's statement was written to recognise that there were increasing legal restrictions on freedom of speech in universities. The amendment weakened the possibility of radical support for free speech in the UCU.

Inaction followed and at the time of writing the UCU still has no academic freedom statement in its aims and objects. But worse may be to come in the UCU's selective support of free speech and academic freedom.

Academic freedom: the freedom that the UCU rejects

Thirty-four candidates for the National Executive Committee of the UCU issued a statement on 16 February 2020 attacking academic freedom (Pendleton 2020). Of course, they dressed up their opposition as a defence of academic freedom. They wanted 'to protect and expand academic freedom while also upholding and safeguarding the rights of transgender, non-binary, intersex and gender diverse colleagues and students'. This seemed like the familiar and false argument that free speech must be restricted to protect vulnerable groups. It is an argument that has gained some support in contemporary victim culture. It remains both historically illiterate and patronising. It ignores the past and present power of free speech when used by the groups they now define as vulnerable to fight for their rights. But they went further and warned (Pendleton 2020):

> In the coming years we are likely to see more attempts to engineer and amplify 'controversies' that will sow confusion and insecurity on campuses. Talks – defended in the name of 'free speech' and 'academic freedom' – by neo-fascists and transphobes will suit that agenda very

well. As trade unionists we must stand firm in denouncing such manufactured controversies.

Going beyond the usual calls for restrictions, the thirty-four happily went along with the view that controversial issues around gender identity and other issues are 'manufactured' and promoted by 'neo-fascists' and 'transphobes'. They are not truly 'free speech' or 'academic freedom' matters. This is a new low for the UCU, which has always defended free speech and academic freedom in a partial way. But worse may be to come as eighteen of the signatories – half of the available positions – were subsequently elected to the NEC.

For this new cohort of trade union leaders, free speech and academic freedom are dangerous concepts that threaten the university as a safe space. Future leaders look like continuing the UCU's indifference to free speech and academic freedom.

The UCU elections in 2021 were a repetition of the 2019 elections. A block of candidates calling themselves 'UCU Commons' stood on a platform that had a 'no debate' policy in their values statement: 'We unequivocally support trans people, whose lives and rights are not up for debate.'[3] They also reissued the anti–free speech candidate statement from 2019. Five members of the block were elected to the NEC. On a positive note, two candidates made pledges about academic freedom. They were not elected.

---

3   UCU Commons (2021): https://ucucommons.org/our-values/.

UCU for academic freedom?

However, the fight for academic freedom inside the UCU took a step forward with the formation of UCU for Academic Freedom (UCU4AF). UCU4AF is an informal group formed by young academics to make the UCU take a stand on academic freedom. In 2020 the UCU4AF wrote to all candidates in the 2020 National Executive elections asking them to pledge their support for academic freedom. Eight of the respondents who made such a pledge were elected (UCU for Academic Freedom 2020a,b 2021). The UCU4AF continued to put pressure on candidates in the UCU election in 2021 and intends to bring a motion to a future UCU Congress on academic freedom.

The future for support for free speech in the UCU remains bleak but, in universities, there is good news on the free speech front. The work of AFAF continues but the most important development is the rise in the number of student free speech societies over the last three years. New free speech societies have been established by students in their universities. The growing list includes Queen Mary University of London and the universities of Bristol, Buckingham, Goldsmiths, Kent and Oxford. Many of the students organising and participating in these societies will be the academics of tomorrow.

Forward with the Free Speech Union?

The launch of the Free Speech Union (FSU) on 26 February 2020 created an organisation that could potentially challenge the indifference and hostility of trade unions to free speech. Founded by writer and journalist Toby Young, with the support of a large team of advisors, its aim was to be a real union and defend through publicity, campaigning and in the courts anyone whose livelihood or reputation was threatened because they exercised their freedom of speech. The FSU soon began to successfully support individuals whose 'offensive' speech had led them to be 'no platformed' or subject to disciplinary proceeding or who were sacked. Its high-profile early cases involved academics, a charity worker, a politician and a radio broadcaster (Free Speech Union 2020). Within a year of its foundation, the FSU had 12 employees and nearly 8,000 members and was expanding overseas (Free Speech Union 2021).

The FSU was initially denounced by those who thought it would be a base for right-wing or left-wing extremist 'nutjobs' to propagate their views.[4] This is a tired criticism from those who fail to recognise how in a therapeutic culture any opinion can be labelled as offensive and denounced. It was fortunate for the FSU that it was formed at a time when 'cancel culture' hit the headlines. Fear of being cancelled encouraged people to join the FSU. There was a debate about whether 'cancel culture' really existed. It does, but it is not new. It is merely a moment when the tendency to ban speakers for dissident opinions that someone finds offensive became near hysterical. The roots

---

4   Simon Kelner has written on these lines: Toby Young's 'Free Speech Union' is illogical – and more to the point, it won't work. *iNews*, 25 February 2020 (https://inews.co.uk/opinion/toby-youngs-free-speech-union-illogical -1891183).

of that hysteria are in contemporary therapy culture. If union members in traditional trade unions – and the FSU – are serious about defending free speech, the first step is to be aware of the therapeutic turn and then stop trading free speech for emotional safety.

Postscript: #Je ne suis pas Samuel

On 16 October 2020, an Islamist terrorist beheaded a teacher of history and geography, Samuel Paty, in a street near his school in the suburbs of Paris. Paty's crime had been to show a selection of *Charlie Hebdo* cartoons of the Prophet Muhammed to his pupils during a civics lesson on the importance of freedom of speech. Politicians, trade unionists and defenders of Enlightenment values throughout Europe condemned the murder. Protests and vigils were held. From the educational trade unions in the UK the response to the murder of a fellow teacher was, however, a deafening silence. The Association of School and College Leaders (ASCL), the Educational Institute of Scotland (EIS), the National Association of Head Teachers, the National Association of Schoolmasters/Union of Women Teachers (NASUWT), and the UCU said nothing, despite appeals for them to condemn the murder and defend free speech.[5] Only the National Education Union (NEU) mentioned the murder of Paty but did not say that he was teaching about the value of free speech, only that he was

---

5   #Je suis Samuel. AFAF Blog, 20 October 2020 (https://www.afaf.org.uk/je-suis-samuel/).

teaching about 'human values'. The silence says how much UK's education unions value free speech – not at all. As the hashtags #Jesuisenseignant and #JesuisSamuel went viral, the UK teacher unions effectively said '#jenesuispas-Samuel'. There is no better example of how far the unions have gone in the retreat from free speech than this. It was a shameful moment in UK trade union history.

11 OFFENCE, HYPOCRISY, AND THE FUNCTION OF DEMOCRACY

David S. Oderberg

Introduction

How should we think of the concept of *offence* in a democratic society with its almost inevitable pluralism of beliefs and allegiances? Recent years have seen most of the Western liberal democracies on a knife-edge of popular instability as a result of issues concerning 'hate speech', 'fake news', 'marginalisation', 'victimisation', 'grievance culture', 'identity politics', and so on. We are now at the point where the literal freedom to 'speak one's mind' about a host of subjects, where that freedom was wholly beyond question in everyone's recent memory, is in danger of destruction – if it is not already in full retreat. At the time of writing, the BBC is removing television programmes from its services due to 'offence',[1] statues are being torn down from our public squares because many consider them an

---

1   Fawlty Towers: John Cleese attacks 'cowardly' BBC over episode's removal. BBC News, 12 June 2020 (https://www.bbc.co.uk/news/entertainment-arts-53020335).

'offensive reminder' of blameworthy aspects of our history,[2] and books and movies are disappearing from libraries and hosting services.[3]

If we are to put up a roadblock against what threatens to destroy democracy altogether – for without the 'freedom to speak one's mind' there can be no democracy, as I will argue – we first need a plausible account of when the causing of offence is and is not acceptable. By 'acceptable' I mean morally, but the account should also indicate how a moral perspective can contribute to considerations as to whether there can be a *legal* right not to be offended. I have no ready-made solution to this problem, but I think much can be said to provide a framework for a solution. At the very least, we should be able to dispel various confusions and diversions that stand in the way of a serious attempt to understand whether there is a 'right not to be offended'. My aim in this short essay is, first, to clear up some of those confusions via a consideration of the relations between offence, insult, and harm. I will then move to a discussion of the legal theorist Jeremy Waldron's position on 'hate speech', followed by a defence of free speech based on what I call the 'deliberation argument', drawing on ideas in the work of James Weinstein and Eric Barendt on the democratic process. Finally, I argue for the conceptual priority of free speech over freedom from offence.

---

2   BLM protestors topple statue of Bristol slave trader Edward Colston. *The Guardian*, 7 June 2020 (https://www.theguardian.com/uk-news/2020/jun/07/blm-protesters-topple-statue-of-bristol-slave-trader-edward-colston),

3   'Gone with the Wind' pulled from HBO Max until it can return with 'historical context'. CNN Business, 10 June 2020 (https://edition.cnn.com/2020/06/10/media/gone-with-the-wind-hbo-max/index.html).

Offence, insult, and harm: conceptual considerations

There has to be a difference between *being* offended and *feeling* offended. Otherwise, there would literally be no such thing as oversensitivity. It must be possible to distinguish between cases where a person may feel they have been offended without justifiably believing they *have* been offended, and cases where a person may feel offended and also believe with justification that they have been offended. To take an extreme and unrealistic example, if you think you have been offended by my complimenting you on your tie, then you are being unreasonable; I have not actually offended you. More realistically, suppose you make a bad move in chess and I, your otherwise friendly opponent, say 'that was a bit of a silly move', it would be plainly oversensitive of you to take offence. You might have hurt feelings, but the proper solution would be for you to toughen up a bit.

Now I will not, as throughout this discussion, offer proposals as to where lines should be drawn in general, especially in the political sphere – our main concern. In the case of feeling versus being offended, as in so much else, context will be important and even decisive as to whether taking offence is justified in a given case. My point is simply that if we do not recognise this elementary distinction, we cannot begin to construct the much-needed protection around free speech in a democracy.

Next, we must distinguish between being *offended* and being *offended against*. To be offended against is to have some harm or damage caused to one, as in 'to be the victim of an offence', with its legal overtones of being the victim of an offender. An offender is not generally thought of as someone who goes around hurting people's feelings but as someone who has traversed a boundary, usually in the criminal law, such that another person has been harmed. One can of course be offended against or harmed without any law being broken: there is no law against breaking promises[4] or taking advantage of someone's good nature.[5] It is the question of harm or damage that matters here. We cannot suppose that hurting someone's feelings – offending them – *ipso facto* damages them. The previous point already anticipates this to a degree: being overly fragile in your reactions to what is said about you can lead to feelings of offence that are not strictly harmful, any more than a glutton is strictly harmed when you refuse to let them have a fourth helping of cake.

The present point goes further, however. Even when a person is justified in taking offence – when they have actually *been* offended – they are not *ipso facto* harmed. Suppose I gratuitously insult you, in a rude and quite unacceptable way, on your appearance. Have you been harmed? Context may well be king. If I wound you with my words in front of your friends or work colleagues, I may well have harmed you by causing intense embarrassment. But it need not be so. If you are perfectly well attired and looking spick and span, although your taking

---

4   Except when those promises meet the condition of being *contracts*.

5   Unless the exploitation amounts to something like gaining a material advantage through deception.

of offence will be merited the proper reaction – as, one hopes, would be the reaction of your friends or colleagues – would be to laugh it off, ignore it or even take pity on me for making a fool of myself rather than of you. By contrast, if I notice that awful ketchup stain on your shirt, which you inadvertently missed in your rush to get dressed, and I highlight it to all the people who can already see it, you will have been harmed in a way that is understandably very difficult to ignore or brush off.

The more egregious cases of harm caused by offence are, of course, well known to lawyers as defamation. Moral theologians of the old school call this sort of action *calumny*, but they also recognise *detraction*, which the law does not. When you calumniate someone you offend them by saying something false that harms their good name, as in defamation; you lower their reputation in the eyes of 'right-thinking people', to use the legal jargon. But you can detract from their reputation as well by saying something *true* about them that is otherwise not public knowledge – something not generally recognised by the courts.[6] Damage to reputation is real and often underestimated; philosophers should give it more attention than they do (see Oderberg 2013 for a lengthy discussion).

So far, we have seen that feeling offended does not entail being offended, and being offended does not entail being harmed. None of this implies any *moral* right to go about offending or risking offence to others. At all times, we think, our speech and manner ought to be

---

6   Except, perhaps, where there is an invasion of privacy.

proper – polite, restrained, sweet tempered, dignified ... all of which, though largely absent from much modern discourse both public and private, still rings true for us when we think about it. This moral injunction, however, rightly does not translate into a general *legal* duty so to behave. The law is far more concerned with egregious harms, those that are relatively public and impactful upon the smooth conduct of social, political, and economic relations. Yet surely there are acts of offence that have just such an effect? When people use their speech to 'wield hate', to vilify individuals and groups, to promote 'extremism',[7] surely people should have a legal right not to be subjected to any of that?

As I have already intimated, if we are thinking of offence in terms of no more than *insult*, then as morally unacceptable as that may be there can be no ground for a *legal* prohibition: hurt feelings, however justified, cannot be actionable in themselves. The law needs to see actual damage, it needs to recognise a matter of public interest, of the protection of the basic rights and liberties of citizenship. Moreover, questions of *intent*, of whether a law against hurt feelings would be void for uncertainty, whether it would be unenforceable – these set up so many roadblocks to the legal prohibition of purely offensive speech that it is a wonder anyone should even contemplate such a law.

---

7   Not involving incitement to violence, which is already a separate criminal matter.

Waldron on 'hate speech'

The more interesting and important issues in current debate, however, concern the *political* dimension of offensive speech. Here, the position of Jeremy Waldron is instructive. He distinguishes between 'causing offence' and 'undermining a person's dignity' (Waldron 2012: 105). While '[p]rotecting people's feelings against offense is not an appropriate objective for the law', argues Waldron, the law should concern itself with 'objective or social aspects of a person's standing in society' (ibid.: 106). Laws against 'hate speech', for Waldron, have the function of 'protecting their [citizens'] dignity and the assurance of their decent treatment in society' (ibid.: 107). It is 'denigration, defamation, and exclusion' (ibid.: 130) against which the law should protect all citizens, so that some individuals or groups do not acquire 'second-class citizenship' (ibid.: 31). If basic citizenship is not protected, Waldron opines, freedom of speech is not worth much in a functioning democracy.

Waldron is right to orient the debate in the direction of the *political* function of speech and whether 'hate speech' should be prohibited in such a context. In other words, it is the public forum of ideas and action, not the private forum of personal feeling, where the serious debate about speech is to be had. Moreover, he is correct to focus on citizenship in a democracy, about which more later. That said, what I feel obliged to call the inconsistency and the *cant* in his discussion is breath-taking. When it comes to the cliched 'crossburning or the daubing of swastikas', he believes 'legislative action is appropriate' (ibid.: 114). But when it comes to the actual presentation of Jesus Christ on a crucifix submerged in urine,[8] we have to 'parse the emotional complex differently in one case from the way we parse it in the other' (ibid.: 115). For 'the primary concern in the hate speech case is with the assault on dignity and the public good of assurance' – meaning assurance of equal dignity as a citizen. Here, Waldron unironically takes it as read that the swastikas and burning crosses constitute 'hate speech' whereas the crucifix soaked in urine does not.

Why the differential treatment? Again, Waldron distinguishes between 'an attack on a body of beliefs and an attack on the basic social standing and reputation of a group of people' (ibid.: 120). Presumably, depicting a crucifix in urine is merely an attack on beliefs, not a denigration of those who hold them. Waldron cannot see any 'group defamation' in public mockery of a religion, only an attack upon the religion's founder, or sacred text, or creed (ibid.: 122–23). If anything, when it comes to religion it seems, for Waldron, that we should be more concerned that 'those who offend others are to be recognised nevertheless as fellow citizens and secured in that status' (ibid.: 130) than that the victims of such offence be secured in *their* democratic status. Waldron's book is full of such artificial distinctions that always seem to go against religious believers: one might as well retort that a public swastika denigrates no man, but merely advertises praise for the 'founder' of National Socialism.

---

8   The notorious prize-winning photograph *Piss Christ* by Andres Serrano.

The lesson of these remarks by Waldron is that when it comes to 'offence' and 'hate speech', if the *democratic* decision is that there be laws protecting citizens against it, then the *democratic* will is that they be applied *fairly* and without playing favourites. Such fairness is quite elusive in most 'liberal democracies'. One might reply on behalf of Waldron that when it comes to beliefs, people have *control*: they can decide whether to be Christian, or Muslim, or observantly Jewish, or of no belief, and so on. One cannot control whether one is ethnically a Jew, or black, or even whether one is homosexual or of one gender rather than another. Also, it might be added, beliefs can be rational or irrational, with or without justification; but one is not irrational for having a certain ethnicity, for example. (Such seems to be the approach to offence of Thomson (1990: 253–59).)

Yet it is hard to see why control or rationality should make a difference to whether offence deserves protection. The objection from control amounts to saying something like, 'If you don't want me to offend you for being Muslim, then just stop being Muslim.' One might as well say, 'If you don't want me to beat you up, don't go strolling in my town.' The mere fact that one has voluntarily taken on a set of beliefs, or a persona or character, and can voluntarily abandon them, gives no ground for denying a putative right not to be offended. Moreover, many beliefs and ideologies are inculcated from childhood and adherence to them is subject to enormous group pressure, in which case the appearance of control would be fairly shallow.

One can, as I have already suggested, control one's *reaction* to offence as well; sometimes, a person just has to 'toughen up', especially when they know that in a pluralist society their beliefs may well be the target of others' mockery and ridicule. Moreover, there are always the so-called 'curtain twitchers' who feign outrage but quite enjoy deep down the feeling of moral indignation. True, and there are ethnic minority members who are tough enough to let racist water flow off their back, yet others who enjoy playing the victim and getting lots of attention. So what? They are hardly the majorities in most groups, giving no basis for an argument *against* the right not to be offended. If I know that a certain person is thick skinned, I may have a bit more latitude with my jokery but it doesn't given me the right to engage in objective rudeness and mockery.

When it comes to rationality, yes a person's beliefs can be not merely false but highly irrational. It's not the mere falsehood that could potentially leave one open to morally legitimate offence – that would be far too strong – but what if the belief really is stupid, asinine, formed by highly irrational means? Linus (of *Peanuts* fame) believes in the Great Pumpkin and waits endlessly in the pumpkin patch for his god to arise and reward the children who believe. I'm sure that if Tim Minchin (a musical comedian and rather vicious atheist) were to meet him, poor Linus would end up dripping with Minchin's spittle and bile. Yet oughtn't the right reaction be one of pity rather than ridicule? And what harm is Linus causing, if his belief is so irrational that hardly anyone would be sucked in by it (as none of the *Peanuts* characters are)? An ugly person might go around preening themselves, but why disabuse a vain person unless they are actually causing mischief? In any case, a rationality requirement on beliefs protected from mockery also seems implausibly strong. The physical analogue would be a person who is reckless or negligent about their own bodily safety. We are all guilty of this sometimes; but if someone walks down a street they know to be dodgy in a hurry to get the bus, that hardly makes it permissible to mug them.

At a minimum, then, if we are to have laws against offensive speech, they should be applied fairly and impartially across the board. Nor should beliefs be treated differently from race or ethnicity, sexual orientation or other 'protected characteristics', as the law characterises them when it comes to equality and non-discrimination.[9] A person's beliefs – not about their favourite ice cream or tomorrow's weather, but concerning their view of the world and what gives meaning to their life – enter as much into their identity as the characteristics they cannot control. If Waldron and others care about a person's status and dignity in a democracy, they should be as concerned about the denigration of such beliefs as about the defamation of a group based on, say, biological characteristics. Of course, beliefs can be discussed, evaluated, criticised, but then those obsessed by race also consider it important to discuss, evaluate and criticise racial characteristics and what they consider to be patterns of behaviour correlated with those. If there is to be a prohibition on 'hate speech', it is hard to see why the discussion of one should be more protected than the discussion of the other.

---

9 Equality Act 2010.

The deliberation argument for free speech in a pluralist democracy

That said, however, I would not want to see society going in this direction if we want to maintain a functioning democracy at the same time. Although there are various arguments for unrestricted free speech in a democracy, I consider what might be called the 'deliberation' argument the most persuasive. (See, for example, Weinstein (2009), although the presentation of the argument is my own.) The idea is that the very essence of democracy is lost if some citizens are prohibited from engaging in the deliberative process broadly construed. By 'deliberative process' I mean the process involving all expressions of opinion and viewpoints that feed into the ultimate decision-making that takes place at the ballot box, in the legislature, in the executive and even in the courts. It is often said, correctly, that the inability to draw a precise line that is superior to all other possibilities does not make it unreasonable to draw lines. There is no good reason why a 30 miles per hour speed limit is superior to 29 or 31, but that is no ground for refusing to draw a line somewhere in the vicinity of what is reasonable. When it comes to the deliberative process, however, there is no way of saying even what *is* a reasonable vicinity. Does the opinion of a high-profile TV pundit 'count' for more than that of my next-door neighbour? Yes in terms of reach and influence, but there is no way of measuring that impact which gives us a sensible boundary between the parts of the deliberative process that count so much that they deserve legal protection from suppression and those that do not.

My point is not simply that there is no *legal* boundary that can sensibly be drawn. Nor is it that for all anyone knows, my neighbour's opinion might end up persuading the local member of parliament, who then plays a pivotal role in passing primary legislation. It is that we have no clue where the *boundary* for impact should be drawn even if my neighbour's opinion never reached the ears of anyone but his own immediate family. The deliberative process, then, *must*, as a matter of conceptual necessity, be drawn broadly enough to encompass expressions of opinion and viewpoint no matter what their source, as long as they are the expressions of a citizen (or group of citizens) of that democracy.

A second way in which the process must be broadly construed is nicely stated by James Weinstein, echoing Eric Barendt (Weinstein 2009: 29, quoting Barendt 2005):

> These two essential components of democracy – popular sovereignty and the individual right of political partici-pation – generate a right of every citizen to participate in the discussion by which the people govern themselves through the formation of public opinion. As Eric Barendt has noted, this speech includes more than 'political speech in the narrow sense' but more generally embraces 'speech concerning the organization and culture of society'.

In other words, the political function of speech that is part of the broad deliberative process need not be *explicitly* political, nor need it have anything to do with political structures in themselves. The 'organization and culture' of society are themselves political – part of the *polis*, to use the hallowed Greek term – so it would be unprincipled to exclude such speech from the process.

Again, it would be arbitrary to suppress what might be called 'cultural speech' that concerned such matters as family life, the relations between the sexes, relations between ethnic, racial, and/or religious groups (assuming the democracy to be 'multicultural', as virtually all of them now are), and for that matter any area of so-called 'private morality'. As to this last, although my own view is that pretty much *every* area of 'private' morality potentially has an impact on public life, the truth of that view is not what grounds the protection. As long as a citizen *believes*, reasonably or not, that some aspect of private morality is a legitimate object of the deliberative process, there is simply no principled way to exclude protection of speech concerning that aspect – whether, note, the speech belongs to the citizen who holds that belief or to anyone *else* who might simply be raising the opinion for *discussion*.

Freedom of speech as prior to freedom from offence

If we think of political speech in this broad sense and as a necessary constituent of the democratic deliberative process, then it is evident that its protection must, in the *order of freedoms* in a democracy, come *prior* to freedom from offence. In other terms, the *positive* freedom to contribute peacefully to the democratic deliberative process

– of which speech is the most important element – must, for the integrity of democracy itself, take moral and legal precedence over the *negative* freedom not to have one's sensibilities, as an individual or as a member of a group, affronted by that speech. Again, being able to speak one's mind about the society in which one lives, to proclaim one's beliefs without fear of suppression or 'cancellation', to use the new term, is the prize whose price is the need for every citizen to 'toughen up' when it comes to public discourse.

How, then, should we respond to the objection that a democratic deliberative process, with untrammelled political speech, can lead to the very violence and oppression that democratic pluralism is supposed to prevent? Untrammelled speech, so the objection goes, opens the door to demagoguery and invites pandering to prejudice. In the extreme, it can lead to the overthrow of democracy itself, as we know all too well from history. It is easy to be overly impressed by what legal theorist Eric Heinze calls 'democracy's well-known paradox of allowing the expression of ideas that would overthrow or weaken democracy' (Heinze 2016: 16). For one thing, ideas do not of themselves overthrow or weaken anything. There has to be *uptake* of those ideas; people have to be *convinced* by them and, moreover, willing to *act* on them. The chain from the expression of a viewpoint to action on that viewpoint of *sufficient strength* to change the very conditions of a democracy – its laws and regulations, the way citizens treat each other, the functioning of entrenched institutions – is a long one, especially if the democracy is mature and well established. There is no necessary connection, either conceptual or causal, between free speech and the weakening or overthrow of any institution.

If anything, the reverse of the 'overthrow' objection is more likely to be true, namely that *banning* speech, however offensive it may be, risks weakening if not totally undermining democracy. In itself it is an authoritarian move, and although there is nothing wrong with authoritarian moves *per se* in a democracy (enforcing the law, for instance) such a ban is of itself likely to undermine core democratic institutions – a free press, the right of peaceful assembly, and freedom of religion among others. Lest there be any doubt about the intrinsic ordering of speech bans towards liberty-reducing effects, consider the 'cancel culture' now prevalent: shadow bans on social media (let alone outright bans)[10]; disinvitations from conferences for 'hateful' words allegedly found in anything from tweets[11] to peer-reviewed academic publications[12]; the shouting down of public speakers and forced abandonment of events[13];

---

10 Twitter appears to have fixed 'shadow ban' of prominent Republicans like the RNC chair and Trump Jr's spokesman. *Vice*, 25 July 2018 (https://www.vice.com/en_us/article/43paqq/twitter-is-shadow-banning-prominent-republicans-like-the-rnc-chair-and-trump-jrs-spokesman).

11 Dawkins disinvited from skeptic conference after anti-feminist tweet. patheos blog, 27 January 2016 (https://www.patheos.com/blogs/accordingtomatthew/2016/01/dawkins-disinvited-from-skeptic-conference-after-anti-feminist-tweet/).

12 Linda Gottfredson's scientific keynote cancelled: Why? *Quillette*, 12 October 2018 (https://quillette.com/2018/10/12/linda-gottfredsons-scientific-keynote-cancelled-why/).

13 Protestors shut down Milo Yiannopoulos event at UC Davis. CNN US, 14 January 2017 (https://edition.cnn.com/2017/01/14/us/milo-yiannopoulos-uc-davis-speech-canceled/index.html).

the 'doxxing' of people on social media for 'wrongthink',[14] often leading to threats of violence against them and their families[15]; and the whole 'ethos of snitching' that pervades the public space.[16] These are the effects of actual laws in place against 'hate speech' and/or of an attitude among the 'woke' that 'hate speech' must be shut down by other citizens if the state will not do it. In short, the 'overthrow' objection to freedom of speech is either (a) a problem for both sides, in which case it cancels out, (b) a problem for neither side, in which case it still cancels out, or (c) a more serious problem for the anti-speech coalition than for the defenders of freedom, in which case the former should not be appealing to it.

A final point against speech bans is that evidence for the priority of speech freedom over hurt feelings lies in the ability to minimise risk and to compensate victims. If speech is banned, it is exceedingly difficult to see how there can be compensation for the loss. If Jones is prohibited from getting his message across, he could be compensated to some extent by allowing Smith to get the same message across in a similar forum, but if *everyone* is banned from getting a

---

14 More than 30 UT students doxxed for crime of being conservative. OJ Media, 13 January 2019 (https://pjmedia.com/news-and-politics/toni-aira ksinen/2019/01/13/more-than-30-ut-students-doxxed-for-crime-of-being -conservative-n63063).

15 Stanford student brags about doxxing conservative journalist. campusre-form, 13 September 2017 (https://www.campusreform.org/?ID=9761).

16 Minneapolis encourages snitching on citizens for 'hate speech' with 'Sha-riah hotline'. Northwest Liberty News, no date (https://northwestliberty news.com/minneapolis-encourages-snitching-citizens-hate-speech-sha riah-hotline/).

particular message across, then how does one compensate for that? No other message will do! By contrast, if speech is untrammelled but offence is thereby risked, the danger can be minimised; and actual victims can be compensated for that danger which is predicated on the freedom to speak. Democratic safeguards can and are built into the system so that the most extreme political speech (short of incitement to violence, of course, which should always be punished) is highly unlikely to gain traction in the legislative and policymaking process. Hence the policies and recommendations contained within it will likely only ever remain hypothetical short of overwhelming public support. Free speech is wholly consistent with public education campaigns against speech that is clearly offensive (in the way Waldron, for example, conceives offence). Such freedom is also consistent with the absence of any specific rights to *particular* platforms for its expression other than those clearly designated as public (or, First Amendment–style, funded partly or wholly by the taxpayer). Needless to say, private spaces will be restricted or not depending on the will of their owners.

Conclusion

Even if you think the free speech/hate speech debate is purely pragmatic rather than a matter of principle, you should think that we ought right now to be erring on the side of freedom. Recent events (Brexit, Trump, the Covid pandemic) have caused or, better, uncovered deep differences in outlook between large segments of society in the

UK, the US and elsewhere. The hostility is palpable, which makes it all the more urgent to open the pressure valve that speech provides. For as we know – and we do not need history to tell us – when serious disagreements exist between people, the alternatives to airing them vigorously but peacefully are always far less attractive and so to be warded off at all costs.

REFERENCES

Aaronson, S. A., and others, Academics and Civil Society Organizations (2019) Liability for user-generated content online, principles for lawmakers. *Santa Clara Law Digital Commons* (scu.edu).

Abrams, D. (2010) *Processes of Prejudice: Theory, Evidence and Intervention.* Manchester: Equality and Human Rights Commission (https://www.equalityhumanrights.com/en/publica tion-download/research-report-56-processes-prejudice-the ory-evidence-and-intervention).

Academics for Academic Freedom (2020) *The Banned List* (https://www.afaf.org.uk/the-banned-list/).

Acharya, B. (2015) Free speech in India: still plagued by pre-modern laws. *Media Asia* 42(3–4): 157–60.

Adelman, L. (2013) The glorious jurisprudence of Thurgood Marshall. *Harvard Law & Policy Review* 7(1): 113–38.

Allen, A. (1870) Balatro. In *Dictionary of Greek and Roman Antiquities* (ed. W. Smith). London: John Murray.

Anderson, E. (2019) *Private Government: How Employers Rule Our Lives (And Why We Don't Talk About It).* Princeton University Press.

ASA/CAP (2017) Depictions, perceptions and harm: a report on gender stereotypes in advertising (https://www.asa.org.uk/ asset/2DF6E028-9C47-4944-850D00DAC5ECB45B.C3A4D9 48-B739-4AE4-9F17CA2110264347/).

ASA/CAP (2020) Using technology for good. Annual Report 2019.

Austin, J. L. (1962) *How to Do Things with Words*. Oxford University Press.

Awan, I. and Zempi, I. (2016) The affinity between online and offline anti-Muslim hate crime: dynamics and impacts. *Aggression and Violent Behavior* 27: 1–8.

Barendt, E. (2007) *Freedom of Speech*, 2nd edn. Oxford University Press.

Barrett, L. F. (2017) When is speech violence? *New York Times*, 14 July (https://www.nytimes.com/2017/07/14/opinion/sund ay/when-is-speech-violence.html).

Bayer, J., Bitiukova, N., Szakács, J., Alemanno, A. and Uszkiewicz, E. (2017) Disinformation and propaganda – impact on the functioning of the rule of law in the EU and its Member States. Report to European Parliament.

Bejan, T. M. (2017) *Mere Civility: Disagreement and the Limits of Toleration*. Cambridge, MA: Harvard University Press.

Benham, L. (1972) The effect of advertising on the price of eyeglasses. *Journal of Law and Economics* 15(2): 337–52.

Berens, V. C. (2014) The Ramesside satirical papyri. Revealing the nature of ancient Egyptian satire (Academia.edu).

Bolloten, B. (2015) Education not surveillance. Institute of Race Relations, 22 October (https://irr.org.uk/article/education -not-surveillance/).

Butcher, J. (2020) Trade unions must stand up for workers' freedom of speech. *Spiked*, 3 May (https://www.spiked-on line.com/2020/03/05/trade-unions-must-stand-up-for-work ers-freedom-of-speech/).

Cady, J. (1976) An estimate of the price effects of restrictions on drug price advertising. *Economic Enquiry* 14(4): 493–510.

Caplan, B. (2018) *The Case Against Education: Why the Education System Is a Waste of Time and Money.* Princeton University Press.

Chakrabarty, N., Roberts, L. and Preston, J. (eds) (2014) *Critical Race Theory in England.* Abingdon: Routledge.

Chisholm, H. (ed.) (1911) Armstrong, Archibald. In *Encyclopædia Britannica.* 2 (11th edn). Cambridge University Press.

Chivers, T. (2020) How racist are you? *Unherd*, 15 January (https://unherd.com/2020/01/why-do-we-spend-millions-on-bs-tests/).

Clark, R. (2007) Advertising restrictions and competition in the children's breakfast cereal industry. *Journal of Law and Economics* 50(4): 757–80.

Coase, R. H. (1974) The market for goods and the market for ideas. *American Economic Review Papers and Proceedings* 64(2): 384–91.

Coase, R. H. (1977) Advertising and free speech. *Journal of Legal Studies* 6(1): 1–34.

Coetzee, A. (1990) Censorship in South Africa. *English in Africa* 17(1): 1–20.

Cowen, N. (2016) Millian liberalism and extreme pornography. *American Journal of Political Science* 60(2): 509–20.

Cowen, N. (2018) Robust against whom? In *Austrian Economics: The Next Generation* (ed. S. Horwitz). Advances in Austrian Economics, Emerald Publishing Limited.

Curtis, M. K. (2000) *Free Speech, 'The People's Darling Privilege': Struggles for Freedom of Expression in American History.* Durham and London: Duke University Press.

de Lange, M. (1997) *The Muzzled Muse: Literature and Censorship in South Africa.* Amsterdam: John Benjamins.

Department for Business, Energy and Industrial Strategy (2020a) Trade union membership. 27 May (https://data.gov.uk/data set/2139dde9-cb3a-43c3-9c93-dc98b91d448e/trade-union -membership).

Department for Business, Energy and Industrial Strategy (2020b) Trade union membership UK, 1995–2019: Statistical Bulletin. 27 May (https://assets.publishing.service.gov.uk/govern ment/uploads/system/uploads/attachment_data/fi le/887740/Trade-union-membership-2019-statistical-bull etin.pdf).

Department for Digital, Culture, Media and Sport (2019) Code of Practice for providers of online social media platforms.

Department for Digital, Culture, Media and Sport and Home Office (2020) Online Harms White Paper: Full government response to the consultation. Cmnd 354.

Dworkin, R. (2013) Rights as trumps. In *Arguing About Law* (ed. A. Kavanagh and J. Oberdiek). Hoboken, NJ: Taylor and Francis.

Ecclestone, K. and Hayes, D. (2019) *The Dangerous Rise of Therapeutic Education* (2nd edn). Abingdon and New York, NY: Routledge.

Edwards, L. (2018) Evidence to House of Lords Select Committee on Regulation of the Internet.

EIU (2020) *Democracy Index 2019.* London: Economist Intelligence Unit (https://www.eiu.com/topic/democracy-index).

Epstein, R. (1987) The fundamentals of freedom of speech. *Harvard Journal of Law and Public Policy* 10: 53–60.

European Commission (2017) Communication on tackling illegal content online – towards an enhanced responsibility of online platforms.

European Commission (2018) Code of practice on disinformation.

Farrior, S. (1996) Molding the matrix: the historical and theoretical foundations of international law concerning hate speech. *Berkeley Journal of International Law* 14(1): 1–99.

Fish, S. (1994) *There's No Such Thing as Free Speech, and It's a Good Thing, Too.* Oxford University Press.

Fiss, J. and Kestenbaum, J. G. (2017) *Respecting Rights? Measuring the World's Blasphemy Laws.* Washington, DC: United States Commission on International Religious Freedom (https://www.uscirf.gov/sites/default/files/Blasphemy%20Laws%20Report.pdf).

Fletcher, W. (2008) *The Inside Story of British Advertising: 1951–2000.* Oxford University Press.

Flynn, D. J., Nyhan, B. and Reifler, J. (2017). The nature and origins of misperceptions: understanding false and unsupported beliefs about politics. *Political Psychology* 38(S1): 127–50.

Foa, R. S. and Mounk, Y. (2017) The signs of deconsolidation. *Journal of Democracy* 28(1): 5–15.

Ford, J. E., Boxer, C. F., Armstrong, J. and Edel, J. R. (2008) More than 'just a joke': the prejudice-releasing function of sexist humor. *Personality and Social Psychology Bulletin* 34(2): 159–70.

Fox, C. (2018) *I STILL find that offensive!* London: Biteback.

Free Speech Union (2021) Newsletter, 28 February (https://freespeechunion.org/newsletters/).

Friedersdorf, C. (2016) The glaring evidence that free speech is threatened on campus. *The Atlantic*, 4 March (https://www.theatlantic.com/politics/archive/2016/03/the-glaring-evidence-that-free-speech-is-threatened-on-campus/471825/).

Gandhi, M. (1921) The Indian National Congress, 29 December.

Gandhi, M. (1922) Statement in the Great Trial, Circuit House, Shahi Bag, Ahmedabad, 18 March.

Glomb, V., Lee, E.-J. and Gehlmann, M. (eds) (2020) *Confucian Academies in East Asia*. Leiden: Brill.

Gray, J. (1992) Advertising bans: administrative decisions or matters of principle? Centre for Independent Studies Occasional Papers 42.

Gurevich, L. (2013) The advertising director as coming attraction: television advertising as Hollywood business card in the age of digital distribution. *Frames Cinema Journal*, May (http:// framescinemajournal.com/article/the-advertising-director -as-coming-attraction-television-advertising-as-hollywood -business-card-in-the-age-of-digital-distribution/).

Haidt, J. (2013) *The Righteous Mind: Why Good People Are Divided by Politics and Religion*. London: Penguin.

Haidt, J. and Haslam, N. (2016) Campuses are places for open minds – not where debate is closed down. *The Guardian*, 10 April (https://www.theguardian.com/commentisfree/2016/apr/10/ students-censorship-safe-places-platforming-free-speech).

Harris, R. and Seldon, A. (2014) [1959] *Advertising in a Free Society*. London: Institute of Economic Affairs.

Hayes, D. (2012) Policing the university. *Spiked*, 1 November (https://www.spiked-online.com/2012/11/01/stop-policing -the-university/).

Heartfield, J. (2017) *The Equal Opportunities Revolution*. London: Repeater Books.

Heinze, E. (2016) *Hate Speech and Democratic Citizenship*. Oxford University Press.

Holland, T. (2019) *Dominion: The Making of the Western Mind.* London: Little, Brown.

House of Commons (2019) Science and Technology Committee: Impact of social media on screen-use on young people's health. House of Commons (parliament.uk).

House of Lords (2018) Select Committee on Communications: UK advertising in a digital age. HL Paper 116. House of Lords (parliament.uk).

Howard, J. W. (2019) Free speech and hate speech. *Annual Review of Political Science* 22(1): 93–109.

Jacobson, H. (1997) *Seriously Funny: From the Ridiculous to the Sublime.* London: Channel Four.

Jaschik, S. (2017) Professors and politics: what the research says. *Inside Higher Ed*, 27 February (https://www.insidehighered.com/news/2017/02/27/research-confirms-professors-lean-left-questions-assumptions-about-what-means).

Kaldor, N. (1950) The economic aspects of advertising. *Review of Economic Studies* 18: 1–27.

Kelling, G. and Wilson, J. Q. (1982) Broken windows: the police and neighborhood safety. *The Atlantic*, March.

Kolb, C. E. M. (1982) The criminal trial of Yugoslav poet Vlado Gotavac: an eyewitness account. *Human Rights Quarterly* 4(2): 184–211.

Langton, R. (2009) *Sexual Solipsism: Philosophical Essays on Pornography and Objectification.* Oxford University Press.

Lasch, C. (1995) *The Revolt of the Elites: And the Betrayal of Democracy.* London: Norton.

Law Commission (2018) Scoping Report on Abusive and Offensive Online Communications.

Lee, T. H. C. (2000) *Education in Traditional China: From the Beginning to ca 1900.* Leiden: Brill.

Liebhafsky, H. H. (1993) A curious case of neglect: Marshall's *Industry and Trade.* In *Alfred Marshall: Critical Assessments* (ed. J. C. Wood). London: Routledge.

Lukianoff, G. and Haidt, J. (2019) *The Coddling of the American Mind: How Good Intentions and Bad Ideas Are Setting Up a Generation for Failure.* London: Penguin.

Macron, E. (2018) Internet of trust, 12 November. The Internet Governance Forum, Paris (https://www.intgovforum.org/multilingual/content/igf-2018-speech-by-french-president-emmanuel-macron).

Mainstream (2019) New campaign to combat extremism in public life.

Mandela, N. (1964) I am prepared to die. Palace of Justice, Pretoria Supreme Court, Pretoria, South Africa, 20 April (http://db.nelsonmandela.org/speeches/pub_view.asp?pg=item&ItemID=NMS010&txtstr=prepared%20to%20die).

Maranto, R., Hess, F. and Redding, R. (eds) (2009) *The Politically Correct University: Problems, Scope, and Reforms.* Washington DC: AEI Press.

Marx, K. (1973) [1885] *The Eighteenth Brumaire of Louis Bonaparte.* In *Selected Works* (K. Marx and F. Engels). London: Lawrence and Wishart.

McCormack, T. (2016) Academic freedom in an age of terror. In *Why Academic Freedom Matters: A Response to Current Challenges* (ed. C. Hudson and J. Williams). London: Civitas.

McCullogh, M. (2020) Liked tweets nearly cost me my university job. *UnHerd*, 29 June 2020 (https://unherd.com/thepost/liked-tweets-nearly-cost-me-my-university-job/).

McGlynn, C. and Ward, I. (2009) Pornography, pragmatism, and proscription. *Journal of Law and Society* 36(3): 327–51.

Mchangama, J. (2011) The sordid origin of hate-speech laws. *Policy Review*, 1 December (https://www.hoover.org/research/sordid-origin-hate-speech-laws).

Meadowcroft, J. (2020) The logic of extremist activism: ideology and the British far-right. Unpublished manuscript, King's College London.

Meadowcroft, J. and Morrow, E. A. (2017) Violence, self-worth, solidarity and stigma: how a dissident, far-right group solves the collective action problem. *Political Studies* 65(2): 373–90.

Merkel, A. (2019) Speech at the general budget debate in the German Bundestag. 27 November, Die Bundesregierung (The Federal Government) (https://www.bundesregierung.de/breg-en/news/kanzlerin-bei-generaldebatte-1699808).

Mill, J. S. (1909) [1848] *Principles of Political Economy with Some of Their Applications to Social Philosophy.* 7th edn (ed. W. J. Ashley). London: Longmans, Green and Co. (https://oll.libertyfund.org/titles/101#Mill_0199_1815).

Mill, J. S. (2006) [1859] On liberty. In *On Liberty* and *The Subjection of Women* (ed. A. Ryan). London: Penguin Books.

Morgan, M. C. (2018) *The Final Act.* Princeton University Press.

Morrow, E. A. and Meadowcroft, J. (2019) The rise and fall of the English Defence League: self-governance, marginal members and the far right. *Political Studies* 67(3): 539–56.

Morsink, J. (1999) *The Universal Declaration of Human Rights: Origins, Drafting, and Intent.* University of Pennsylvania Press.

Mueller, M. L. (2015) Hyper-transparency and social control: social media as magnets for regulation. *Telecommunications Policy* 39(9): 804–10.

Newell, S (2016) Paradoxes of press freedom in colonial West Africa. *Media History* 22(1): 101–22.

Newman, D. (2013) British colonial censorship regimes: Hong Kong, Straits Settlements and Shanghai International Settlement, 1916–1941. In *Silencing Cinema: Film Censorship around the World* (ed. D. Biltereyst and R. V. Winkel). New York: Palgrave Macmillan.

Newman, J. H. (2008) [1889] *The Idea of a University Defined and Illustrated in Nine Discourses Delivered to the Catholics of Dublin*, Gutenberg Press edition (http://www.gutenberg.org/files/24526/24526-pdf.pdf).

Oderberg, D. S. (2013) The morality of reputation and the judgment of others. *Journal of Practical Ethics* 1: 3–33.

Oderberg, D. S. (2018) *Opting Out: Conscience and Cooperation in a Pluralistic Society*. London: Institute of Economic Affairs.

Ofcom (2020) Decisions on recent programmes featuring David Icke and Eamonn Holmes.

Office for Students (2018) Freedom of speech (https://www.officeforstudents.org.uk/advice-and-guidance/student-wellbeing-and-protection/freedom-of-speech/what-should-universities-and-colleges-do/).

Oldenburg, R. (1989) *The Great Good Place: Cafes, Coffee Shops, Community Centers, Beauty Parlors, General Stores, Bars, Hangouts, and How They Get You Through the Day*. Paragon House.

Oldenburg, R. (2000) *Celebrating the Third Place: Inspiring Stories about the 'Great Good Places' at the Heart of Our Communities*. Marlowe & Company.

Packard, V. (1957) *The Hidden Persuaders*. New York: D. McKay.

Pendleton, M. (2020) UCU election candidates' statement on academic freedom and trans inclusion. Medium. 16 February (https://medium.com/@mark.pendleton/ucu-candidates-statement-on-academic-freedom-and-sex-and-gender-b652802782f8).

Pluckrose, H. and Lindsay, J. (2020) *Cynical Theories: How Universities Made Everything About Race, Gender, and Identity – And Why This Harms Everybody.* London: Swift Press.

Popper, K. (1945) *The Open Society and Its Enemies.* London: Routledge.

Ramsay, I. (2006) Globalization, the Third Way and Consumer Law: The Case of the UK. In *Consumer Protection in the Age of the 'Information Economy'* (ed. J. K. Winn). Aldershot: Ashgate.

Rand, A. (1971) The cashing in; the student rebellion. In *The New Left: The Anti-Industrial Revolution.* New American Library 47.

Rashdall, H. (2010) [1895] *The Universities of Europe in the Middle Ages,* Vol. I. Cambridge University Press.

Redish, M. H. (2017) Commercial speech and the values of free expression. *Cato Institute Policy Analysis,* 19 June, #813 (https://www.cato.org/publications/policy-analysis/commercial-speech-values-free-expression).

Reicher, S. (2020) UK scientists condemn 'Stalinist' attempt to censor Covid-19 advice. *The Guardian,* 8 May (https://www.theguardian.com/world/2020/may/08/revealed-uk-scientists-fury-over-attempt-to-censor-covid-19-advice).

Riley, E. (2020) Leave-supporting firefighter sacked from post on union's national executive after speaking at pro-Brexit rally sues for unfair dismissal. *Daily Mail,* 6 February (https://www.dailymail.co.uk/news/article-7974111/Firefighter-sues-union-unfair-dismissal-sacked-speaking-Brexit-rally.html).

Roman, L. and Roman, M. (2010). *Encyclopedia of Greek and Roman Mythology.* New York: Infobase Publishing.

Shattock, J. (ed.) 2019 *Journalism and the Periodical Press in Nineteenth-Century Britain.* Cambridge University Press.

Shiell, T. C. (2019) *African Americans and the First Amendment: The Case for Liberty and Equality.* New York: SUNY Press.

Skoczylis, J. (2015) *The Local Prevention of Terrorism: Strategy and Practice in the Fight against Terrorism.* London: Palgrave Macmillan.

Skoczylis, J. and Andrews, S. (2019) A conceptual critique of Prevent: can Prevent be saved? No, but ... *Critical Social Policy* 40(3): 350–69.

Slater, T. (2019) Free speech university rankings. *Spiked*, 24 February (https://www.spiked-online.com/free-speech-university-rankings/).

Slater, T. (2020) Cancel culture is not about the powerful. *Spiked Online*, 13 July (https://www.spiked-online.com/2020/07/13/cancel-culture-is-not-about-the-powerful/).

Smith, G. (2020) Online Harms White Paper – Response to Consultation.

Snowdon, C. (2017) *Killjoys: A Critique of Paternalism.* London: Institute of Economic Affairs.

Steindl, C., Jones, E., Sittenthaler, S., Traut-Mattausch, E. and Greenberg, J. (2015) Understanding psychological reactance: new developments and findings. *Zeitschrift für Psychologie* 223(4): 205–14.

Stigler, G. J. (1971) The theory of economic regulation. *The Bell Journal of Economics and Management Science* 2(1): 3–21.

Strossen, N. (2018) *HATE: Why We Should Resist It with Free Speech, Not Censorship.* Oxford University Press.

Thomas, D. C. (2001) *The Helsinki Effect: International Norms, Human Rights, and the Demise of Communism*. Princeton University Press.

Thomas, M. (2003) Mark Thomas has had enough of the SWP. *New Statesman*, 19 May (https://www.newstatesman.com/node/157659).

Thomson, J. J. (1990) *The Realm of Rights*. Harvard University Press.

Trades Union Congress (2018) WorkSmart (https://www.getworksmart.co.uk/about).

Trades Union Congress (2020a) Stress (https://www.tuc.org.uk/union-reps/health-safety-and-well-being/stress).

Trades Union Congress (2020b) Bullying at work (https://www.tuc.org.uk/resource/bullying-work).

Trades Union Congress (2020c) Well-being (https://www.tuc.org.uk/union-reps/health-safety-and-well-being/well-being).

Trades Union Congress (2020d) Mental health (https://www.tuc.org.uk/resource/mental-health-and-workplace).

Trades Union Congress (2020e) Tackling the far-right (https://www.tuc.org.uk/TacklingFarRightResource).

Trantidis, A. (2016) *Clientelism and Economic Policy: Greece and the Crisis*. Routledge Advances in European Politics 126. Routledge.

Trantidis, A. (2017) Is government contestability an integral part of the definition of democracy? *Politics* 37(1): 67–81.

Trantidis, A. and Cowen, N. (2020) Hayek versus Trump: the radical right's road to serfdom. *Polity* 52(2): 159–88.

Trepczynski, S. (2020) White silence on social media: why not saying anything is actually saying a lot. *CBS News*, 3 June (https://

www.cbsnews.com/news/white-silence-on-social-media-why-not-saying-anything-is-actually-saying-a-lot/).

Turley, J. (2020) How 'silence is violence' threatens true free speech and public civility. *msn news*, 29 August (https://www.msn.com/en-us/news/politics/how-silence-is-violence-threatens-true-free-speech-and-public-civility/ar-BB18uJGS).

UCU for Academic Freedom (2020a) UCU for Academic Freedom (https://ucu4af.wixsite.com/website-2).

UCU for Academic Freedom (2020b) Blog (https://ucu4af.wixsite.com/website-2/blog).

UCU for Academic Freedom (2021) How (https://ucu4af.wixsite.com/website-2/how).

Universities UK (2014), *External Speakers in Higher Education Institutions*. London: Universities UK.

University and College Union (2009) Statement on academic freedom. 1 January (https://www.ucu.org.uk/academicfreedom).

University and College Union (2012) Academic Freedom: a guide for early years staff (https://www.ucu.org.uk/media/5128/Academic-freedom--a-guide-for-early-careers-staff/pdf/Academic_freedom_leaflet.pdf).

University and College Union (2015) The Prevent duty: a guide for branches and members (https://www.ucu.org.uk/media/7370/The-prevent-duty-guidance-for-branches-Dec-15/pdf/ucu_preventdutyguidance_dec15.pdf).

University and College Union (2017a) Academic freedom in 2017 (https://www.ucu.org.uk/academic-freedom-in-2017).

University and College Union (2017b) UCU Congress 2017 (https://www.ucu.org.uk/article/8798/Business-of-the-Education-Committee-2017#40).

Van Rooyen, J. C. W. (1978) *Publikasiebeheer in Suid-Afrika*. Cape Town: Juta.

Van Rooyen, J. C. W. (1987) *Censorship in South Africa*. Cape Town: Juta.

Veblen, T. (1899) *The Theory of the Leisure Class*. New York: Macmillan.

Vermeule, A. (2017) A Christian Strategy. *First Things* (https://www.firstthings.com/article/2017/11/a-christian-strategy).

Wager, N., Armitage, R., Christmann, K., Gallagher, B., Ioannou, M., Parkinson, S., Reeves, C., Rogerson, M. and Synnott, J. (2018) Rapid evidence assessment: quantifying the extent of online facilitated child sexual abuse: report for the Independent Inquiry into Child Sexual Abuse.

Waldron, J. (1987) Mill and the value of moral distress. *Political Studies* 35(3): 410–23.

Waldron, J. (2012) *The Harm in Hate Speech*. Harvard University Press.

Walker, S. (1994) *Hate Speech: The History of an American Controversy*. Lincoln and London: University of Nebraska Press.

Weale, S. (2018) Safe spaces used to inhibit free speech on campuses inquiry finds. *The Guardian*, 27 March (https://www.theguardian.com/education/2018/mar/27/safe-spaces-used-to-inhibit-free-speech-on-campuses-inquiry-finds).

Weinstein, J. (2009) Extreme speech, public order, and democracy: lessons from the masses (pp. 23–61) and An overview of American free speech doctrine (pp. 220–32) In *Extreme Speech and Democracy* (ed. I. Hare and J. Weinstein). Oxford University Press.

Woodhouse, J. (2020) Gambling advertising: how is it regulated? House of Commons Library Briefing Paper 7428 (https://res

earchbriefings.files.parliament.uk/documents/CBP-7428/CBP-7428.pdf).

Wu, F. T. (2011) Collateral censorship and the limits of intermediary immunity. *Notre Dame Law Review* 87: 1.

Zempi, I. (2017) Researching victimisation using auto-ethnography: wearing the Muslim veil in public. *Methodological Innovations* 10(1): 1–10.

Zivi, K. (2012) *Making Rights Claims: A Practice of Democratic Citizenship*. Oxford University Press.

ABOUT THE IEA

The Institute is a research and educational charity (No. CC 235 351), limited by guarantee. Its mission is to improve understanding of the fundamental institutions of a free society by analysing and expounding the role of markets in solving economic and social problems.

The IEA achieves its mission by:

- a high-quality publishing programme
- conferences, seminars, lectures and other events
- outreach to school and college students
- brokering media introductions and appearances

The IEA, which was established in 1955 by the late Sir Antony Fisher, is an educational charity, not a political organisation. It is independent of any political party or group and does not carry on activities intended to affect support for any political party or candidate in any election or referendum, or at any other time. It is financed by sales of publications, conference fees and voluntary donations.

In addition to its main series of publications, the IEA also publishes (jointly with the University of Buckingham), *Economic Affairs*.

The IEA is aided in its work by a distinguished international Academic Advisory Council and an eminent panel of Honorary Fellows. Together with other academics, they review prospective IEA publications, their comments being passed on anonymously to authors. All IEA papers are therefore subject to the same rigorous independent refereeing process as used by leading academic journals.

IEA publications enjoy widespread classroom use and course adoptions in schools and universities. They are also sold throughout the world and often translated/reprinted.

Since 1974 the IEA has helped to create a worldwide network of 100 similar institutions in over 70 countries. They are all independent but share the IEA's mission.

Views expressed in the IEA's publications are those of the authors, not those of the Institute (which has no corporate view), its Managing Trustees, Academic Advisory Council members or senior staff.

Members of the Institute's Academic Advisory Council, Honorary Fellows, Trustees and Staff are listed on the following page.

The Institute gratefully acknowledges financial support for its publications programme and other work from a generous benefaction by the late Professor Ronald Coase.

Other books recently published by the IEA include:

Islamic Foundations of a Free Society
Edited by Nouh El Harmouzi and Linda Whetstone
Hobart Paperback 183; ISBN 978-0-255-36728-8; £12.50

The Economics of International Development: Foreign Aid versus Freedom for the World's Poor
William Easterly
Readings in Political Economy 6; ISBN 978-0-255-36731-8; £7.50

Taxation, Government Spending and Economic Growth
Edited by Philip Booth
Hobart Paperback 184; ISBN 978-0-255-36734-9; £15.00

Universal Healthcare without the NHS: Towards a Patient-Centred Health System
Kristian Niemietz
Hobart Paperback 185; ISBN 978-0-255-36737-0; £10.00

Sea Change: How Markets and Property Rights Could Transform the Fishing Industry
Edited by Richard Wellings
Readings in Political Economy 7; ISBN 978-0-255-36740-0; £10.00

Working to Rule: The Damaging Economics of UK Employment Regulation
J. R. Shackleton
Hobart Paperback 186; ISBN 978-0-255-36743-1; £15.00

Education, War and Peace: The Surprising Success of Private Schools in War-Torn Countries
James Tooley and David Longfield
ISBN 978-0-255-36746-2; £10.00

Killjoys: A Critique of Paternalism
Christopher Snowdon
ISBN 978-0-255-36749-3; £12.50

Financial Stability without Central Banks
George Selgin, Kevin Dowd and Mathieu Bédard
ISBN 978-0-255-36752-3; £10.00

Against the Grain: Insights from an Economic Contrarian
Paul Ormerod
ISBN 978-0-255-36755-4; £15.00

Ayn Rand: An Introduction
Eamonn Butler
ISBN 978-0-255-36764-6; £12.50

Capitalism: An Introduction
Eamonn Butler
ISBN 978-0-255-36758-5; £12.50

Opting Out: Conscience and Cooperation in a Pluralistic Society
David S. Oderberg
ISBN 978-0-255-36761-5; £12.50

Getting the Measure of Money: A Critical Assessment of UK Monetary Indicators
Anthony J. Evans
ISBN 978-0-255-36767-7; £12.50

Socialism: The Failed Idea That Never Dies
Kristian Niemietz
ISBN 978-0-255-36770-7; £17.50

Top Dogs and Fat Cats: The Debate on High Pay
Edited by J. R. Shackleton
ISBN 978-0-255-36773-8; £15.00

School Choice around the World … And the Lessons We Can Learn
Edited by Pauline Dixon and Steve Humble
ISBN 978-0-255-36779-0; £15.00

School of Thought: 101 Great Liberal Thinkers
Eamonn Butler
ISBN 978-0-255-36776-9; £12.50

Raising the Roof: How to Solve the United Kingdom's Housing Crisis
Edited by Jacob Rees-Mogg and Radomir Tylecote
ISBN 978-0-255-36782-0; £12.50

How Many Light Bulbs Does It Take to Change the World?
Matt Ridley and Stephen Davies
ISBN 978-0-255-36785-1; £10.00

The Henry Fords of Healthcare: …Lessons the West Can Learn from the East
Nima Sanandaji
ISBN 978-0-255-36788-2; £10.00

An Introduction to Entrepreneurship
Eamonn Butler
ISBN 978-0-255-36794-3; £12.50

An Introduction to Democracy
Eamonn Butler
ISBN 978-0-255-36797-4; £12.50

Other IEA publications

Comprehensive information on other publications and the wider work of the IEA can be found at www.iea.org.uk. To order any publication please see below.

Personal customers

Orders from personal customers should be directed to the IEA:

IEA
2 Lord North Street
FREEPOST LON10168
London SW1P 3YZ
Tel: 020 7799 8911, Fax: 020 7799 2137
Email: sales@iea.org.uk

Trade customers

All orders from the book trade should be directed to the IEA's distributor:

NBN International (IEA Orders)
Orders Dept.
NBN International
10 Thornbury Road
Plymouth PL6 7PP
Tel: 01752 202301, Fax: 01752 202333
Email: orders@nbninternational.com

IEA subscriptions

The IEA also offers a subscription service to its publications. For a single annual payment (currently £42.00 in the UK), subscribers receive every monograph the IEA publishes. For more information please contact:

Subscriptions
IEA
2 Lord North Street
FREEPOST LON10168
London SW1P 3YZ
Tel: 020 7799 8911, Fax: 020 7799 2137
Email: accounts@iea.org.uk

Notes

Notes

Notes

Notes